The Tomb of English People

Visit: www.tombofengland.co.nz

The Tomb of English People

Duncan Balmer

Pentland Books
Durham · Edinburgh · Oxford

By the same author:

The Investment Jungle

(HarperCollins*Publishers New Zealand*)

STOP! Do Not Invest In Residential
Property . . . (Third Opinion Limited)

© Duncan Balmer 2000

First published 2000
by Third Opinion Limited
Suite 163, 2a Byron Avenue
Takapuna, Auckland
New Zealand

This edition
published in 2001 by
Pentland Books
1 Hutton Close
South Church
Bishop Auckland
Durham

British Library Cataloguing in Publication Data.
A catalogue record for this book is available
from the British Library.

ISBN 1 85821 897 7

Typeset by George Wishart & Associates, Whitley Bay.
Printed and bound by Antony Rowe Ltd., Chippenham.

To:

Avril, Charlie and A.J.

You've all got some English blood in your veins;

be proud of it.

Contents

	Page
Preface	9
Introduction	13

Part One - Causes

Chapter 1 - A Brief History of England, Britain and the United Kingdom ... *19*

Chapter 2 - A Brief History of the British Empire and Commonwealth ... *37*

Part Two - Effects

Chapter 3 - The English Legal and Political System ... *47*

Chapter 4 - The English Language ... *78*

Chapter 5 - The English Contribution to Sport ... *91*

Chapter 6 - Other English Contributions ... *99*

Part Three - Myths and Reality

Introduction ... *117*

Chapter 7 - Ireland and Scotland ... *119*

Chapter 8 - The Colonies and Empire ... *135*

Conclusion ... *143*

Appendices

A - Reigns of the Kings and Queens of England ... *152*

B - Certain Clauses of Magna Carta, 1215 ... *154*

C - Brief Notes on Some Famous English Battles ... *159*

Notes ... *176*

Bibliography ... *177*

Index ... *178*

PREFACE

Since this book concerns itself with the history and achievements of "the English", a moment spent defining the term "English" might be appropriate. The Oxford English Dictionary defines the word English as "of England . . . by birth, descent or naturalization". Therefore, notwithstanding the fact that this story is dominated by Anglo-Saxons, "English" does not mean *only* Anglo-Saxon. The English are mongrels, being in the first place an admixture of Angles, Saxons and Jutes with an indeterminable amount of "indigenous" Celt. Ever since, this original dough has been leavened (and quite possibly improved) by Welsh, Scots and Irish, Danes, Normans, Jews, Huguenots from France, other Europeans, and more recently by Africans and Asians (in England) or by indigenous races abroad.

Therefore, the term "English" includes not only all Anglo-Saxons living in England or anywhere else in the world, but also any non-Anglo-Saxons living in England who feel that they have become "English" through naturalization and long domicile (thus "the English nation" comprises all persons - whatever their colour, current citizenship or country of domicile - who are English by birth, descent, or naturalization).

Some people who are only partially English may not wish to acknowledge that particular part of their heritage, of course. Similarly, some "pure" or part-Anglo-Saxons scattered around the world may simply consider themselves to be Americans, or Canadians, or Australians, or Kiwis, etc., and may not have any interest in acknowledging their English ancestry or origins. This is fine by me, because I would not wish to force "Englishness" upon anybody who does not want it: one might say that some people are born English, some achieve Englishness . . . but none should have Englishness thrust upon them!

Racism is an out-dated, repugnant and morally bankrupt doctrine, and I do not adhere to its "philosophies". Whilst the avowed intention in these pages is to accentuate the positives in English history (to offset to some degree the exasperating tendency of the English to denigrate themselves), it is hoped that this book will not be adjudged racist; it is not intended to be. I seek only to demonstrate in these pages that the English have a lot to be proud of, not that they are necessarily superior to any other race or group of people.

A few definitions: *British* does not mean English (nor vice versa), British means from England or Scotland or Wales; *Britain* consists of England, Scotland and Wales; the *United Kingdom* does not mean Britain, it means Britain plus Northern Ireland. Whilst on the subject of geography, I have tended to use modern names rather than those current at the time of incidents discussed (thus Holland rather than the United Provinces, for example). "India" generally means modern Pakistan, India and Bangladesh, unless otherwise stated. The terms "English-speaking countries", "Anglo-Saxon countries" and "Anglo-American countries" are used interchangeably and, depending on the context, mean England, Scotland, Wales, the island of Ireland, the United States of America, Canada, South Africa, Australia and New Zealand. These expressions are simply three short-hand ways of listing the countries just mentioned, and no offence is intended to any citizen of any of these countries who may not be, or may not like to be referred to as, Anglo-Saxon.

I should like to thank my father, Tom Balmer, for proof reading the manuscript, and for his constructive criticism. I would also like to thank my wife, Avril Balmer, for carrying more than her fair share of our child-rearing burden, whilst I was otherwise occupied. Thanks to my wife and to her nephew Ian McLoughlin for their Irish perspectives. Thanks also to my Scottish friend Jen Hughes, for her comments. All opinions are mine, not theirs.

I have tended to use the male pronoun throughout - this has not been because I object to political correctness (although I do), but merely because I find it easier and less clumsy to write "Englishman" than to write "Englishman/woman" or "Englishperson". My apologies to anyone offended by this - but, hey, get a life!

INTRODUCTION

The Ancient Greeks used to say of their heroes:

The whole earth is the tomb of heroic people,
and their story is not graven only on stone over clay,
but abides everywhere,
woven into the stuff of other people's lives.

Likewise, England's story abides everywhere, woven into the stuff of other people's lives.

England's story is most intricately woven into the fabric of her former colonies and dominions, of course, influencing everything from their political and judicial systems, to the side of the road on which most of them still drive. But England's influence spreads way beyond her former colonies and dominions. England has, for example, provided the whole world with a universal language, and with a universal datum against which all locations and all times are measured (the Greenwich Meridian and Greenwich Mean Time, also known as "Universal Time"). Englishmen invented some of the best loved international sports, and standardized the rules of many others. England initiated the industrial revolution. And so on.

Thus, every time a jury convenes in a Canadian courtroom, or an American President is impeached; every time a New Zealander goes to an Anglican church, or an Australian casts a vote; every time an Irishman drives to work, or an Indian catches the train; every time a Chinese aircraft plots its position, or a Peruvian ship charts a course; every time a South African asks a German "Do you speak English?", or a Russian (searching for a shared language) asks a Korean the same question; every time a Superbowl final kicks off in America, or an Algerian kid kicks a football around his back yard, and every time a Bolivian boy scout pitches his tent, or a Danish down-and-out shuffles into his local Salvation Army soup kitchen; a direct and specific link can be traced back to England and her history.

This book is about that history, and is divided into three parts. Part 1, entitled "Causes", provides some historical background, covering the distinctly different political, geographical and ethnic entities "England", "Britain", the "United Kingdom" and the "British Empire". It should be noted that Part 1 does not purport to be an exhaustive, academic history of these entities, but is simply intended to provide a broad overview to the interested layman. Those readers seeking a definitive history of the four "home" countries or of the British Empire will need to consult any of the more scholarly tomes available on those subjects, such as those mentioned in the bibliography. Inevitably, many battles on land and at sea have punctuated England's story, and brief details of some of the most significant of these battles can be found at Appendix C, for those of a bellicose persuasion!

Part 2, entitled "Effects", deals firstly with English constitutional history and law, which have had such profound effects upon those countries which have come under the direct influence of England at one time or another. Part 2 continues with an examination of the contributions which the English people have made to the broader world, in a series of chapters covering such subjects as the English language, sport, the industrial revolution, Greenwich Mean Time and the Greenwich Meridian, and so on.

Part 3, entitled "Myths and Reality", examines the twaddle talked about the English by some Irish, Scottish and other myth-peddlers, and attempts to redress the balance of their rhetoric a little.

The recurring theme throughout this whole book is that England has a highly significant place in the world's history, and that all those who wish to acknowledge their Englishness have a great deal to be proud of.

Stop reading now if those thoughts get up your nose.

Part One

Causes

Chapter 1

A BRIEF HISTORY OF ENGLAND. BRITAIN AND THE UNITED KINGDOM

Celtic times to 1801

England

At the time of the Roman invasion, the land which is now known as England was the domain of the Celts, who were a tall, light-haired race of people from north-western Germany and the Netherlands. The Celts had themselves arrived in the few centuries before Christ, and had imposed themselves as an aristocracy upon the pre-Celtic tribes of Britain and Ireland. The Celts had no territorial or feudal structures, and at the time of the Roman invasion they remained entirely tribal in character, and were perpetually at war with one another. However, some Celts did maintain close political communication with their kinsmen across the English Channel, and when they heard that Julius Caesar was marching upon their neighbours, sent ships and men to assist. This was one of the causes of Caesar's invasion of Britain, along with his needs of booty, and political kudos back home.

Caesar's invasions of 55 and 54 BC were ineffectual affairs, and Roman invasion proper can be dated to Claudius' conquest of 43 AD. In their usual style, the Romans did not indiscriminately slaughter and displace the indigenous population, but rather cultivated and seduced the existing hierarchy into a symbiotic relationship with Rome. Thus, the land remained almost exclusively populated by Celtic Britons during the Roman occupation (particularly to the north and west), and so it remained through the waning and disintegration of the Western Roman Empire.

The Anglo-Saxons (whose incursions commenced in the fifth century AD) were somewhat more thorough than their Roman predecessors. They raped and pillaged their way around their new homeland in the traditional manner, assimilating some Celts into their own blood-lines, and pushing others out to the extremities of the country, into what are now known as Scotland, Wales and Cornwall. Their vigorous and profane style of immigration also extinguished city life, the Christian religion and the Romano-Celtic language.

Eventually, out of the mess, three great Anglo-Saxon kingdoms emerged - Northumbria, which was the first of the three to exert a broad influence over much of what could by then be termed "England" (mid seventh century), then Mercia (mid eighth century), and lastly Wessex (mid ninth century). Under Alfred the Great's descendants, Wessex was destined properly to unite the whole of England for the first time, by overturning the ninth and tenth century Danish occupation of the "Danelaw" (the north-east and east of England), until that mighty achievement was itself overturned by the Danish King Canute, who claimed the whole of England into his Danish empire, in 1016.

Add some Viking blood (in particular Danish blood, by way of the said Danish occupations, and Norwegian blood by way of their occupation of the north-west at the time of the Danelaw), and add a little bit of Norman blood (the Normans were also Danes, by the way, not French) and essentially you have the final version of that high-achieving mongrel, the Anglo-Saxon.

The restoration of the Saxon king Edward the Confessor (1042-1066)[1], and the desperate struggles of his successor Harold in 1066, first fending off a Norwegian invasion at Stamford

Bridge, then failing to fend off the Norman one at Hastings, can be quickly passed over here.

Similarly, the succeeding 419 years of Norman, Angevin/Plantagenet[2], Lancastrian and Yorkist sovereignty need only be briefly touched upon here, although some political and constitutional developments of the first magnitude which took place during that period will be discussed in Chapter 3. For now it is only necessary to mention a few seminal events, such as England's loss of Normandy in 1204, and of the rest of her French possessions, bar Calais, by the end of the Hundred Years' War (1337-1453). The combined effects of these (apparent) disasters was the development of a national identity and a national language, with all things French (including the French language) coming to be seen by the nobility as "foreign" and "enemy". Also noteworthy was the catastrophic Black Death of the late 1340s, which carried off between a third and a half of Western Europe's population, and gave rise in England to a degree of social emancipation, since labour consequently became an extremely scarce commodity. The pointless tragedy known as the Wars of the Roses, which started two years after the end of the Hundred Years' War, is also not especially germane to the theme of this book, except insofar as it eventually raised up to the throne of England an obscure Welsh nobleman by the name of Henry Tudor.

Almost coincident with Henry VII's seizure of the Crown (1485), the Americas were (re) - discovered (1492). The accident of geography which had until that moment meant that England had always been somewhat on the periphery of things suddenly turned to our advantage. All of a sudden, England lay right in the middle of the western world, instead of at one end of it.

This fact has shaped England's history ever since, leading as it did to her development as a naval power naturally inclined to colonization and foreign commerce.

The Sixteenth Century

By the turn of the sixteenth century, the feudal and horizontally-stratified English society, with its two masters in London and Rome, was dissolving. It was doing so under the influence of many things, including the discovery of new ocean trade routes and the New World, the nationally unifying but personally emancipating effects of a national cloth trade, the consequent rise of an English middle class, the intellectual liberation engendered by the Renaissance, and the invention of the cannon and the printing press. In its place was slowly developing a vaguely democratic, self-confident nation-state, with a Crown-Parliament axis at its core, rather than (as remained the case in France and Spain) a Crown-Church axis. The constitutional developments that had brought England to such a situation by this time are discussed in Chapter 3.

The eleventh century movement to spiritually and politically reform the Catholic Church in Rome (spearheaded by Pope Gregory VII) had given the papacy political importance throughout Europe. As is well known, in due course the Catholic Church fell back into evil and profane ways, and by the late fifteenth century the Renaissance was giving voice to criticism of its idolatry, extortionism and other manifold failings. The teachings and opinions of men such as Luther, Erastus and Colet sowed the seeds which the reforming Henry VIII so vigorously reaped, and it is surely ironic that the man who in his younger years wrote a book attacking Luther, and who was consequently granted the title "defender of the faith" by the pope, should later be the chief instrument of the destruction of pontifical authority in England.

The immediate cause of Henry VIII's attack on the Catholic Church (which was a struggle for the supremacy of the State over a Roman Church manipulated by foreign rivals, not for Protestantism over Catholicism) was the question of his marriage to Catherine of Aragon, whom he wished to be rid of. Pope Clement VII's refusal to grant his wish infuriated Henry, and outraged his countrymen at just the time when strong feelings about national sovereignty and criticism of the Catholic Church's many failings were abroad. Henry therefore broke with Rome (1534), with the assistance of Parliament (which sat for seven years and passed the required legislation). In playing its part in these proceedings, Parliament greatly increased its own importance, and established in the minds of Englishmen the previously unthinkable concept of the State's supreme authority to make any laws which it chose within its own borders. Henry became the supreme head of the Church in England (which was still a Catholic one, and was only slowly transformed into a Protestant one during Elizabeth I's reign), and the Reformation was secured against counter-attack by the wise policy of selling the Church's confiscated property to large numbers of laymen, who thereby developed a vested interest in the status quo.

Henry VIII created the Royal Navy, and personally insisted upon the novel design feature of mounting cannons within the bodies of his battleships, to be run out through port-holes cut through their hulls. The great historian Trevelyan describes the shattering broadsides which the English Navy was thus able to deliver as "the operation of war to which, more than to any other, British maritime and colonial power owe(d) their existence".

Between Henry VIII and Elizabeth I (i.e. the years 1547-1558), England was brought low through misrule by Edward VI's protectors and by Mary I (in thrall to her husband Philip of

Spain). So much so, in fact, that in Elizabeth's early years the rivalry of Spain and France was all that saved England from conquest, because neither country could countenance the other gaining control of her.

In due course England regained her strength under Elizabeth I, to such a point that she was no longer susceptible to invasion. She sent an army to assist the Scottish Protestants, and thereby secured the Scottish Reformation and unknowingly laid the groundwork for the later union of the two countries. Elizabeth became confident enough to knight Francis Drake following his successful circumnavigation of the globe (which was taken as a direct affront by the Spaniards whom he had plundered on the way), and eventually to execute Mary, Queen of Scots. Sir Francis' destruction of the Spanish Armada which was sent in response (1588) was a seminal event for the whole of Europe, securing as it did the survival of the Dutch Republic, the emancipation of France from Spain and above all, demonstrating that mastery of the seas (if not yet the lands beyond them) had passed from Spain and Portugal, to England.

Wales

Early Anglo-Saxon occupation of Wales was largely thwarted by the Welsh mountains, and so the job of invading Wales was left to Edward the Confessor (1042-66), and in particular to the early Anglo-Normans (say, 1066-1199), in the guise of the "Marcher Lords" and their private armies. In time, the warlike Lords Marcher (who acted more on their own account than on that of the English Crown) subdued all of Wales save the "Principality" of the Llewelyn family, centred around Mount Snowdon.

Thus at the start of the thirteenth century Wales was two distinct entities; the territory of the Lords Marcher (the majority of the land area), and the Principality of the Llewellyns in the north-west. Llewellyn the Great and his grandson Llewellyn ap Gruffydd re-conquered a fair amount of west Wales from that base, but the latter over-stepped the mark against Edward I (1272-1307), who crushed the Llewellyns' movement, divided up the Principality into English-style shires (by the Statute of Wales 1284), and declared his son the first Prince of Wales. At the end of the thirteenth century, therefore, Wales was partly the direct domain of the King (the Principality), and partly the domain of the troublesome Lords Marcher.

One further flowering of Welsh independence occurred briefly under Owen Glendower in the early fifteenth century, but died with him, and in 1535 Wales was formally annexed under Henry VIII (himself of Welsh origin) on terms of equality with England. Henry abolished both Principality and Marcher Lordships, and replaced them with counties governed in the English style, and represented in the English Parliament.

The Seventeenth Century

In 1603, with the death of Elizabeth I, the English Crown passed to James VI of Scotland, by right of his senior claim (all Henry VIII's children had died without heirs, his brother had predeceased him without heirs, and his eldest sister, Margaret, who had married James IV of Scotland, was James' great-grandmother). James had, by the time of his accession to the English throne, been King of Scotland for 36 years.

Unfortunately, James' ignorance of his new realm gave rise to many difficulties. For example, at the turn of the seventeenth century the Scottish Parliament was still a cypher, doing little more than recording what was being laid down from on high, whereas the English Parliament already held an altogether more important position in England (see Chapter 3). Thus James was wont to fulminate dangerously about the outrageous insolence of the squires and lawyers who made up the English Commons, whenever they dared try to circumscribe his divine authority.

By 1603, England was a thoroughly Protestant country, but a significant minority of Catholics remained, and James mismanaged the resultant "Catholic question" badly. James' Catholic policy wavered from one extreme to the other, and it was during one of his swings of policy against Catholics that a group of exasperated Jesuits formulated the famous gunpowder plot of 1605 in a bid to kill both King and Parliament. The outrage against Catholics which the gunpowder plot implanted into the breast of the ordinary Englishman remained a constant theme throughout the Stuart era (1603-1688).

The Royal Navy was allowed to decay over this period, and England consequently lost influence abroad. The deep resentment against the Stuarts which this caused amongst English mariners and merchants was responsible in no small part for the defection of the bulk of the Royal Navy to the Parliamentary cause during the first civil war.

During the early years of Charles I's reign (1625-1649), some ill-advised military and naval expeditions against France and Spain brought the monarchy into disrepute, particularly since they were used by the King as excuses for such illegal activities as un-Parliamentary taxation, arbitrary imprisonment and martial law. The Petition of Right (1628) conceded that these activities were illegal but as Trevelyan says, "the Petition of Right, like Magna Carta, was the beginning, not the end, of a struggle for the principles it enunciated".

Charles I dispensed with parliaments in 1629, and commenced

his habit of dismissing judges if and when they dared to interpret the law impartially. He gradually removed every constitutional check upon his actions, and thereby put himself and his authority into stark juxtaposition with the opinion of Parliament, which considered the law to have an independent existence of its own, above the King.

In order to understand the period 1642-1660, it is necessary to appreciate that there were two English civil wars; the first was between the Crown and a mixed Parliament of Anglicans and Puritans (which Parliament won), and the second was between a largely Anglican Parliament and the Puritan Army (which Parliament lost). After the first civil war (1642-1646), caused by Charles' despotism and his zealous promotion of the High (Anglican) Church at the expense of all other churches and forms of worship, Charles lost all authority to Parliament and fled to Scotland. After the second civil war (1648), caused by Parliament's foolish refusal to grant religious toleration to the Puritans who had physically fought and won the first civil war, Parliament lost all authority to the Army, which in due course declared the monarchy and the House of Lords abolished, executed the King, and declared England to be a Commonwealth.

Cromwell's Protectorate became increasingly authoritarian, imperialistic and expensive, and therefore increasingly unpopular as time went on. His death (at a time when he was inching towards the restoration of the monarchy in his own person), and the succession to the Protectorate by his unworthy son Richard, made the eventual Restoration of Charles II inevitable.

Ironically, by 1660 it seemed to the broad mass of Englishmen that if the nation was to regain its "ancient" liberties the monarchy must be restored, because custom and political fact had by then developed a suitably self-regulating relationship (when not abused) between Crown, Parliament, and Nation, based upon English common law. The need to recall a Stuart monarch was thus apparent to the Parliament of 1660, which duly did just that, in the person of Charles II. An important point to note is that Parliament recalled the King - not the other way round - and when doing so, Parliament was careful to ensure that the powers of the restored monarchy were circumscribed, so as to bring the relationship between Crown and State back into some sort of equilibrium. Parliament was also understandably keen to reduce the power of the army, and did so through the effective expedient of disbanding it!

Unfortunately, in the half-French Charles II (1660-1685), England had found itself a traitor for a monarch. For his own selfish dynastic reasons he made a public agreement with Louis XIV to attack Holland (whose defeat would have been disastrous to English maritime interests, and highly beneficial to France). Worse than this, he also made a secret agreement with Louis to be supplied with French money and soldiers, so that he could declare himself a Catholic, and promote Catholic interests in England. The follies and treachery of Charles II's reign allowed France to cement for itself a place in Europe which only a military genius of the calibre of the Duke of Marlborough could dislodge.

James II (1685-1688) was no better, except that he was honest enough to declare his Catholicism openly. He came into immediate conflict with an Anglican Parliament whose support for the concept of monarchy was exceeded only by its rabidly anti-Papist feelings. The fear of a Catholic Restoration was boiling to a fever pitch amongst the general populace at this same time, as they became aware of the horrors being inflicted by Jesuits in France upon the Protestant Huguenots. Moderate Anglicans and Puritans increasingly saw that they were going to have to subordinate their ancient enmities to the necessity of controlling the King, and hopes for a resolution of the problem began to focus upon the Protestant William of Orange and his wife, Mary, James' daughter. An attempt by James to humiliate seven Anglican bishops, foiled by a jury which found them not guilty of the seditious libel of which James had accused them, brought matters to a head, and Parliament sent an invitation to William of Orange to come across and take the Crown. James' army immediately started to dissolve into factions, his nerve faltered, and he fled to France rather than do battle against William.

The great constitutional significance of the Glorious Revolution of 1688 is discussed in detail in Chapter 3. Here, it need only be mentioned that this latter revolution and the period which followed gave to England (and Scotland) both freedom and efficiency; brought to the fore the two party system of politics that had just recently developed; and tipped the balance of power permanently in favour of Parliament.

In 1694 the Bank of England was established, and the financing of the capitalist development of the world's resources began to centre upon England. At the moment when England was fast becoming the financial capital of the world, the Glorious Revolution also brought England political leadership of a Protestant European alliance against Louis XIV, who was busily engaged in his doubly offensive attempts to conquer Europe, and restore the Stuarts in England and Scotland.

Scotland

Lowland (south-eastern) Scotland had already been invaded and occupied by the Anglo-Saxons (specifically, the Northumbrians) by the mid sixth century AD, and a king of Northumbria had

29

given his name to a town established on a prominent rock beside the River Forth, called "Edwin's Burgh".

To the north, Kenneth MacAlpin emerged out of the chaos of Pictish-Celtic warfare in 844 AD to unite the highland parts of Scotland, and during the ninth and tenth centuries the Danes to the south and the Vikings to the west cut lowland Scotland off from England, and the whole of Scotland off from Ireland. This turned Scotland in upon itself, and by the beginning of the eleventh century, the Anglo-Saxon part of Scotland was acknowledged as the territory of the Scots. Upon the securing of the lowlands to the Crown of Scotland, there then ensued an important transformation of the Scottish Crown and the Scottish body-politic; they slowly transformed from being north-western, tribal and Celtic into being south-eastern, feudal and Anglo-Norman - accelerated by Scottish/English inter-marriage, and the immigration of Anglo-Norman families such as those later known as the Bruces, the Balliols, and the Stuarts.

England and Scotland were almost united in 1290 in the person of the future Edward II, who was betrothed to the young heir to the Scottish throne (Margaret, "the Maid of Norway"), but she died before the marriage could take place, and the chaos which ensued threw up William Wallace and, later, the politically flexible Robert Bruce. A combination of Bruce's statesmanlike qualities and England's later distraction with the Hundred Years' War in France ultimately secured the independence of Scotland, until its voluntary relinquishment in 1707.

The exigencies of England's struggle against Catholic Europe in the time of Elizabeth I laid the groundwork for the eventual unification of Scotland and England, because England could no longer afford the distraction of continual warfare in the north. Unification became more inevitable when the Scottish nobles, backed at a critical juncture by an English fleet and army, were successful in securing John Knox's Scottish Reformation, and ultimately the flight of Mary, Queen of Scots to England.

From 1603, England and Scotland were ruled as separate realms by the same monarchs, and this fact inevitably lent a certain logic to the idea of eventual union. Cromwell's temporary rule of a combined English and Scottish nation during his Protectorate, which briefly brought to Scotland the substantial benefit of free trade with England, advanced the idea further. The Restoration of Charles II sundered the free trade arrangements, and the Glorious Revolution restored Scotland to a state of practical independence of England. Nevertheless, by the first years of the eighteenth century it was clear to statesmen on both sides of the border that there were benefits to be had from the union of the two countries. Scotland was desperately poor, and was in urgent need of the economic security and material assistance which could only come from free access to the markets of England and all her colonies. For her part, England desired safeguards against rebellion in her rear by the Jacobites (the faction seeking the restoration of the Stuart monarchs), since she had turned her thoughts elsewhere.

The Act of Union (1707) effected the union of England and Scotland on 1st May 1707, under the name of Great Britain. The Scottish Parliament passed the treaty in January 1707, and the English Parliament passed it soon thereafter. The two Crowns and Parliaments became one, the Protestant succession was secured, Scottish law and religion were left unmolested, and free trade was established throughout the new realm and its dominions.

The Eighteenth Century

By the date of the death of Queen Anne in 1714, England had been united with Scotland, the Duke of Marlborough had completely destroyed the power and prestige of Louis XIV in the War of the Spanish Succession, and Great Britain had acquired its vital and portentous footholds in the Mediterranean, at Gibraltar and Minorca.

The eighteenth century was the century when the modern form of England's parliamentary system was cemented into place (even if the degree of true representation was still woeful, since the franchise was only held by landowners, and because of the existence of "rotten boroughs"). Nevertheless, England had a Prime Minister, Cabinet, ministries, and adversarial political parties, as she still has today. It was also the century of the industrial revolution, of enclosure of open fields and common land, of rapidly rising population, and of fantastic military success for England (as part of Great Britain), helped in no small way by the absence of the Scottish distraction at her rear. It was the century when the movement towards empire picked up pace substantially, with the acquisition of Gibraltar, Minorca, Canada, India, and Australia. Great Britain's imperial activities in the eighteenth century are discussed in more detail in Chapter 2.

Eighteenth century England was a place of corrupt and unrepresentative parliaments, but nevertheless a place conducive to enterprise and discovery. Foreign Protestant refugees were importing specialist industrial skills; capital was beginning to accumulate in England at a prodigious rate; free trade existed from one end of Britain to the other (as it did not in Germany, Italy or France); science was held in high regard; and foreign markets were developing and becoming available which would be capable of taking any quantity of anything which English industry might care to manufacture. Conditions were thus set fair for the industrial revolution, which commenced in the second half of the century.

After the failure of the second Jacobite rebellion, of 1745, Scotland settled her "Highland question" (anachronistic tribalism and feudalism in the Highlands), by establishing the Highland chiefs as landlords of their lands, with their clansmen relegated to the position of tenants.

By the end of the Seven Years' War against France (1756-1763), the imperial pretensions of England's only serious rival had been completely destroyed in India (Plassey), North America (Quebec), Europe (Minden), and at sea (Quiberon Bay). Britain's North American victories during the war removed the French threat to the American colonies, which amplified the colonists' feelings of independence, and their resentment of British trade restrictions and taxation.

Over the first twenty years of his reign, King George III (1760-1820) gradually wrested political control back into the Crown's hands, but Britain's failure in the American War of Independence brought him into disrepute, and his system of personal government to an end. Royal prerogative was replaced, permanently, by Parliamentary supremacy, Cabinet government, and the party political system.

The industrial revolution effectively commenced in the reign of George III, coincident with a rapid rise in population and assisted by the construction of a canal network. Men and women flooded into Lancashire, Merseyside, Tyneside, Clydeside, the Black Country, South Wales and London, to serve the rapidly growing industrial businesses.

And so the eighteenth century ends with Britain astride a rapidly growing empire, about to crown her glory with her victories at Trafalgar and Waterloo, but experiencing growing pains domestically, and suppressing much needed parliamentary and social reform at home, for fear of plebeian revolution.

Ireland

The Celtic island of Ireland, like the north-west of England, was invaded by the "Outer Line" Vikings (from Norway) in the ninth and tenth centuries AD. Following the defeat of the Vikings by Brian Boru at Clontarf in 1014, the Viking influence waned, and some progress was made towards the creation of a centralised state under a single High King.

In 1169, Richard de Clare ("Strongbow"), the Earl of Pembroke, invaded Ireland (nominally on behalf of Henry II), assisted by some Cambro-Norman (Welsh-Norman) compatriots. He and succeeding generations of Anglo-Normans carved out a firm control of the immediate environs of Dublin (the "Pale"), and a loose control of large parts of the rest of the island.

In the style of successive waves of people who have invaded China, the Anglo-Norman aristocracy in Ireland became increasingly Gaelicised over time (even within the Pale) so much so that, by the time of the Reformation, they were found to be largely hostile to the Protestant cause. This, and the fact of Ireland's closeness to England and continental Europe, with its consequent potential as a base for English malcontents or foreign enemies, gave Irish affairs a renewed relevance in Tudor England.

Following a series of revolts, which arose from religious differences and the English policy of introducing settlers from Britain, Gaelic resistance was worn down until, in 1601, the last

Gaelic stronghold, Ulster, was brought under control.

Cromwell's subjugation of Ireland in the mid-seventeenth century was brutal and extensive, and it completed the transference of land east of the Shannon from Irish to British ownership: a process which had been going on since the Tudor and early Stuart times. The native gentry were destroyed, leaving the priests as the only remaining natural leaders of the native people.

At the Battles of the Boyne (1690) and Aughrim (1691), the struggle for supremacy was finally settled in favour of the English, at which time large numbers of Anglo-Irish and Gaelic-Irish fled abroad.

A tradition of radical Irish patriotism developed in the late eighteenth century, fostered by the American and French revolutions, culminating in an insurrection in Ireland in 1798 by the United Irishmen. This rebellion was crushed, and the idea formed in the mind of the British Prime Minister William Pitt the Younger that a full union of the British and Irish Parliaments was the best solution to the "Irish question". Pitt's idea was that a union would strengthen the connection between the two countries, and provide greater opportunities for Irish economic development. Through the blatant purchase of sufficient votes in both Parliaments, the Irish Parliament voted to abolish itself and thereafter seek representation for Ireland at Westminster, and the British Parliament acquiesced. The Act of Union 1801 thus created a full parliamentary union between Britain and Ireland, under the title of the United Kingdom of Great Britain and Ireland.

Review

Thus, by 1801 the United Kingdom of Great Britain and Ireland was one nation and, incredible as it would have seemed at that moment, greater military and diplomatic glories than those already achieved were yet to come. The United Kingdom already stood astride a massive empire; had almost complete control of the world's seas and oceans; had become the world's richest nation; and had already won for herself a wide moral authority because of her (albeit imperfect) democratic institutions and customs.

And at her core, providing the bulk of her population, economic activity, and military power, stood England.

Chapter 2

A BRIEF HISTORY OF THE BRITISH EMPIRE AND COMMONWEALTH

Preamble

As has already been stated, the discovery of the Americas at the end of the fifteenth century suddenly placed England in the middle of the world, rather than at one end of it.

In the sixteenth century, what could be considered to be England's first unconscious steps towards establishing a maritime empire were taken by the likes of Sir Francis Drake (who circumnavigated the globe in 1577-80), and Sir Walter Raleigh (who sired a still-born colony in Virginia in 1587, and sailed up the Orinoco).

The Seventeenth Century

The story really begins, though, in the seventeenth century. The process of assembling an empire was a haphazard one, with colonial activities generally initiated by companies or individuals, rather than with any malice-aforethought on the part of the English Crown.

Competition with France and Portugal in particular, and commercial ambition, drove things forward, and led to the establishment of trading posts by the East India Company in India and on the Straits of Malacca from 1600 onwards. India, of course, became the jewel in the British Crown, and many mighty fortunes were made there - most notably that of Thomas

Pitt, grandfather of Pitt the Elder (leader of the nation during the Seven Years' War) and great-grandfather of Pitt the Younger (British Prime Minister during the Napoleonic Wars). The first successful English colony in North America was established at Virginia in 1607, and Cromwell sent an expedition to capture Jamaica in 1655 (this event is noteworthy as England's first deliberate act of empire building). The first permanent settlement on the African Coast was made in the Gambia River in 1661. Charles II's government annexed a group of Dutch colonies on the American mainland in 1664, thus putting together an unbroken chain of English colonies from Maine to the Carolinas, and the Hudson's Bay Company established itself in Canada from about 1670.

By this time, England's strength already lay in her large manufacturing base, and as she gained in maritime power as well, so she was well placed to quickly outstrip her closest maritime and commercial rival, Holland. Thus by the end of the Stuart period (1688), England had far out-stripped Holland in maritime and commercial influence, and was matched only by Louis XIV's France in military power.

The Eighteenth Century

The eighteenth century began with the War of the Spanish Succession (1701-1713), which was fought on the one hand by Louis XIV, who wished to claim the whole Spanish inheritance for his grandson (and who, into the bargain, had irritated the English by recognizing the Old Pretender as James III). His protagonists were an alliance of the Habsburg emperor, the English and the Dutch. Louis was eventually brought to terms, and the terms which are relevant to England (Great Britain by time the war was concluded) involved the acquisition of Gibraltar and Minorca, plus Nova Scotia, Newfoundland and the

Hudson Bay territory. The Treaty of Utrecht, which concluded the war, marked the end of French imperialism until the coming of Napoleon, and it also marked the unmistakable arrival of Great Britain as a maritime, commercial and financial "superpower".

There followed a period of consolidation, until the advent of the Seven Years' War (1756-1763). This war was also disastrous for France, and a brilliant success for Great Britain. France's influence in India and North America was effectively ended, she was thrown back within her own borders in Europe, and she was swept from the sea - all at the hands of British forces.

In India, the acquisition of Bengal by Clive, following his victory at Plassey (1757) converted the British East India Company from an armed trading corporation into a regional power. France's continued trouble-making in the area forced the pace of further British expansion, and in 1784 Pitt's India Act established Cabinet control over the activities of the company. British India grew like Topsy, as the protection offered by Britain to various Indian states (from foreigners and from each other) took on a momentum of its own, and could not ultimately be stopped except at India's natural geographic boundaries. The character of Britain's activities in India slowly changed from arbitration to acquisition as, particularly in the earlier years, it was demonstrated time and time again that peace throughout the disintegrating Moghul empire would only come through the suzerainty of a single dominant power.

Britain's only significant set-back in the eighteenth century was in America, where the famous dispute over taxation without representation ultimately led to the dissolution of the first British empire. It should be noted that the group of foreign possessions which remained, and which was subsequently added to and consolidated as described below, is sometimes termed the *second* British empire, to differentiate that empire from the "empire" which was lost as a result of the American War of Independence.

Meanwhile in the Pacific, Captain James Cook and others were going about their business, settling Australia, and charting New Zealand for the British Crown.

The Nineteenth Century

The nineteenth century marks the full flowering of the second British empire, marked by a change in the methods of administration and control, from the haphazard arrangements of the seventeenth and eighteenth centuries to a sophisticated system of central control, through the Colonial Office (commenced 1801).

During the French Revolutionary and Napoleonic wars (say, 1793-1815, from Britain's perspective) Britain's lead over the rest of Europe in colonisation and trade increased immeasurably. The Royal Navy kept enemy merchant fleets off the ocean highways, and her apparent naval invincibility was indelibly imprinted upon the mind of the world at Trafalgar. Various treaties during or at the end of the wars gave Britain Trinidad, Ceylon, Tobago, Mauritius, St. Lucia and Malta.

The Cape of Good Hope was acquired in 1806, and the Southern African interior was thence opened up by Boer and British pioneers under British control.

Sir Stamford Raffles acquired Singapore in 1819; Canadian settlements in Alberta, Manitoba and British Columbia extended British influence across to the Pacific; New Zealand and Hong Kong were settled in the 1840s; and control was greatly extended in India. The Indian Mutiny of 1857 caused the British government to assume direct government of that country the following year, and in 1877, Queen Victoria took the title "Empress of India".

Various less notable acquisitions and extensions of influence were made, and by the end of the nineteenth century the British Empire comprised nearly one-quarter of the world's surface, and over one-quarter of the world's population.

The Twentieth Century

The Boer War (1899-1902) led to the last major accretion of territory, in the annexation of the Transvaal and the Orange Free State in 1902.

World War I led to a more formal recognition of the special status of the dominion countries (Canada, Australia, New Zealand and South Africa, at that time) leading to the Statute of Westminster in 1931 effecting the equality of the United Kingdom and its then dominions, consisting of the four countries just mentioned plus Ireland and Newfoundland.

In Ireland, the Easter uprising of 1916 was suppressed, but in 1919 the "war of national independence" erupted, which was concluded in 1921 by an Anglo-Irish peace treaty granting independence to 26 of the 32 counties of Ireland (as the Irish Free State), and granting the 6 northern counties their own Northern Ireland Parliament, as a continuing part of the United Kingdom.

The imperial conference of 1926 declared that the self-governing dominions were to be regarded as "autonomous communities within the British Empire, equal in status, in no

41

way subordinate one to another in any aspect of their domestic or external affairs, though united by a common allegiance to the Crown, and freely associated as members of the British Commonwealth of Nations".

The Statute of Westminster provided that no law made by any particular parliament (in practice, the Parliament of the United Kingdom) would become the law of any dominion "otherwise than at the request and at the consent of that dominion".

Nationalism amongst African and Asian countries grew particularly after World War II, with the effect that, starting with India in 1947, independence was progressively granted these nations also.

THE COMMONWEALTH

The Commonwealth evolved out of Britain's imperial past, and is now an association of free and sovereign states sharing a common working language, and similar systems of law, public administration and education.

In 1867, Canada became the first colony to be transformed into a self-governing dominion. Australia followed suit in 1901, New Zealand in 1907, South Africa in 1910, and the Irish Free State in 1922. The Imperial Conference of 1926 defined the nature of the British Commonwealth, and the Statute of Westminster formalized and defined the dominion nations' statuses. The Statute was immediately adopted by Canada, Newfoundland (then separate from Canada), the Irish Free State and South Africa. Australia adopted the Statute in 1942, and New Zealand in 1947.

India gained independence from the United Kingdom in 1947,

and in 1949 she was admitted as the first republican member and, as a corollary, the principle of "allegiance to the Crown" by members of the Commonwealth was abrogated. At the same time, the word "British" was removed from the title of the organization. The removal of an insistence upon allegiance to the Crown allowed many other nations to join, where they might otherwise not have done.

Ghana achieved independence in 1957 and became the first majority ruled African member. During the 1960s the Commonwealth expanded rapidly, taking in members from Asia, Africa, the Caribbean and the Pacific.

The Commonwealth currently has a little over 50 freely associated members, with the aims of advancing democracy, human rights, and sustainable economic and social development.

Part Two

Effects

Chapter 3

THE ENGLISH LEGAL AND POLITICAL SYSTEM

Preamble

The subjects to be discussed in this chapter - English common law, the English legal system, and English parliamentary democracy - might seem somewhat daunting to the casual reader, and if such subjects cannot be faced then the reader should turn now to the conclusion to this chapter (page 76), and continue from there. However, it is hoped that the reader will persevere, because these three things profoundly affect the lives of more than one and a half billion people, which makes them fundamental to the theme of this book.

Introduction

England was perhaps stimulated to develop constitutional arrangements earlier in her history than most other countries through having to put up with so many foreign monarchs. She has had Danish, Norman, Scottish, Dutch and German kings over the last one thousand years (not to mention Welsh ones), and as time went by the English nobility and the English people came to exercise a growing degree of power over them - and they did so somewhat earlier and more enduringly than their contemporaries elsewhere. They did this through a constitution which ultimately led their nation (and the nations which England has most directly influenced) down a very different path from those of all their contemporaries abroad, to the considerable credit of all those who caused this to happen.

Those who live today under one of the English constitution's many offspring include the citizens of the world's largest democracy - India - and the citizens of the world's most powerful country - the United States.

English Common Law

Common law is the jumble of precedents, cases and decisions which slowly develops over time out of the judgments of courts interpreting a standard set of laws across a land. In contrast to civil (Roman) law, it is fundamentally a law of practice rather than theory. As late as the late nineteenth century, English common law was still primarily the product of judges applying custom and common sense to legal matters, rather than the product of legislators.

Alfred the Great (871-899) codified all Saxon and Danish laws as they stood in his time in England, and he is therefore sometimes considered the founder of English common law. Nevertheless, the honour is more usually given to Henry II (1154-1189), under whose jurisdiction "modern" English common law started to develop. It evolved out of the proceedings of Henry's royal courts, as he and other Norman kings sought to wrest legal authority from their nobles. Henry laid down writs enabling his subjects to bring many kinds of action in the King's courts, rather than through local feudal or ecclesiastical courts, and this led to the development of a consistent case law, which applied throughout the land. Various Norman and Angevin kings (when short of funds) would be obliged to promise and re-promise that English common law would have precedence throughout England, and by the reign of Edward I (1272-1307), this was actually so.

The English Constitution

The English constitution is made up of "laws proper", and conventions. Conventions have not actually been laid down by law, but have simply achieved permanency through long usage, or force of habit. Examples of conventions would include Cabinet being collectively responsible to Parliament for the conduct of the executive; that the party which commands a majority in the House of Commons is entitled to form a government; and that all courts are bound by Acts of Parliament. There are no laws which say these things must be so: they are merely conventions.

The United Kingdom's lack of a written constitution is perplexing to some people, especially some foreigners, and yet it has its merits. A typically English air of vagueness and imprecision pervades the United Kingdom's constitutional arrangements, and this vagueness allows the constitution to bend to new circumstances, and generally adapt without need of violent insurrection (e.g. the French Revolution), or lengthy political process (e.g. the processes involved in amending the Constitution of the United States). Since the United Kingdom's constitution is not written down anywhere, it can be modified smoothly and simply by ordinary Acts of Parliament, by judges making ordinary decisions in their courts, and by changing conventions - and can thus be modified in ways which written constitutions cannot.

English constitutional history is essentially fifteen hundred years long, since the institutions and customs which the Anglo-Saxons brought to England largely survived the Danish and Norman conquests. Thus, the Anglo-Saxons' customs and institutions can legitimately be thought of as the "gene pool" of the modern constitution. Be that as it may, the four great landmarks in English constitutional history date from later times. These are Magna Carta (1215); the Petition of Right (1628); the Bill of Rights (1688); and the Act of Settlement (1701). It is no coincidence that three of these four landmarks were laid down within seventy-five years of each other, all connected in one way or another with the execrable royal surname "Stuart".

However, let us approach the matter of English constitutional history in a logical manner, and consider these four landmarks at the appropriate moments. When considering these landmarks, and most of the other constitutional developments discussed below, the reader should remember with respect that they did not come easily, and that many Englishmen risked and/or suffered torture, ruin and death to achieve them.

Saxon England

It is not fanciful to attribute England's constitutional uniqueness to her Anglo-Saxon roots. In England many elements of Anglo-Saxon custom survived the Danish and Norman conquests, and therefore survive to this day, whereas on the European continent Saxon laws and customs were in due course completely extinguished by feudal systems.

The Saxons were a Germanic people, of course, and they brought with them a number of things worthy of note in the present context. Firstly, they brought their native tradition that rulers should take counsel from their great men, and act upon it. Secondly, they brought their tradition of remote self-government, under the occasional close scrutiny of a normally distant king. The territorial units known as shires, hundreds and vills, and the shire courts and hundred courts, were employed extensively by Anglo-Saxon kings as instruments of governmental and judicial administration. This helped English kings rule more effectively than those of most other European countries of the day, but the flip-side of this arrangement was that it was always more difficult for English kings to entirely ignore the opinions of the great men and functionaries who ran these administrative units, even if they wished to. Thirdly, the Anglo-Saxons brought with them their assumption of the fundamental trustworthiness of the law-abiding freeman, which is apparently unique to Anglo-Saxon tradition. After the Norman conquest, the sworn testimony of the law-abiding freemen of the district would become fundamental to the administration of justice, and to the carrying out of the King's government. Fourthly, the Saxons brought with them their ancient Germanic custom that a king should be disobeyed if he acts unlawfully.

The role of the Anglo-Saxon King was to maintain the law rather than amend it and, although the notion slowly developed that crime might be an offence against the King rather than solely a matter between the interested parties, there was no real agreement that this entitled Anglo-Saxon kings to *make* law. They were there more to administer it, and to force people at loggerheads to submit to jurisdiction. As an aside, the mechanism used was known later as *peine forte et dure*, and consisted of crushing a recalcitrant defendant with heavy weights, and feeding him stale bread and stagnant water on alternate days. Horrifyingly, this sanction was last applied as late as 1726, when an unfortunate by the name of Burnswater refused to plead on a charge of murder; *peine forte et dure* was applied (to the tune of about 200 kg.), and he then came to his senses and pleaded "not guilty". To add insult to injury (or, one might say, extreme prejudice to extreme pressure), it is recorded that Burnswater was duly convicted and hanged. *Peine forte et dure* was finally abolished in 1772, and replaced by an assumption of guilt if no plea was entered. It was not until 1827 that a refusal to plead was taken to be a "not guilty" plea.

Feudalism, imported into England by the Normans, added some important elements to the English constitutional system. The concept of land tenure at the pleasure of a superior, in return for certain services (usually military), fixed the idea of government through contractual obligation in men's minds, and generally heightened the relevance of law in that sphere. However, despite the permanency of some of its *effects*, and in contrast to the general experience on the continent and in other parts of the world, the feudal system *per se* gradually withered in the face of growing central government by English kings.

Henry II's empire encompassed England, Ireland and most of France. This stimulated the development of local administrations, and in England (where Henry spent less than half of his 35 years in power), government became increasingly complex and bureaucratic. This fact, together with the novel proceedings of his royal courts, which he sent out to the shires to administer his justice from afar, has led to him being regarded as the founder of English common law.

The Jury System

The "jury-of-verdict" is an Anglo-Norman invention, although two customs from Anglo-Saxon times may lie at the root of England's jury system, and may also explain why juries generally have twelve members. Firstly, in Anglo-Saxon jurisdictions criminals were presented for trial by twelve thegns (landholders). Secondly, Danish towns (within the Danelaw) often had twelve "law-men" as their principal officers, governing in committee.

Whether or not the above facts have any bearing on the matter, it was Henry II who, by about 1179, had given life to the real embryo which would become trial by jury. Henry's jury system allowed the King's courts to slowly monopolize the administration of justice throughout England, at the expense of the myriad feudal and manorial courts which administered their own more arbitrary forms of justice. In matters of disputed land ownership, a plaintiff could henceforward call twelve witnesses who were aware of the local facts of the case, to testify before the King's justices as to who had the better claim to the land. Note that the twelve persons were witnesses, rather than impartial hearers of the case, at this stage. At about the same time, a second kind of jury (also of twelve sworn witnesses) was empowered to present before the courts those of their neighbours who had allegedly committed crimes.

The right to trial by jury (as opposed to the concept of juries *per se*) looks directly back to Clause 39 of Magna Carta (1215), which states:

> No free man shall be arrested or imprisoned or disseised [dispossessed] or outlawed or exiled or in any way victimised, neither will we attack him or send anyone to attack him, except by the lawful judgment of his peers or by the law of the land.

By coincidence, Pope Innocent III abolished trial by ordeal throughout (western) Christendom in the same year as Magna Carta which, in England at least, seemed to indicate the need for a second or "petty" jury to try the truth of accusations (the "jury-of-verdict"). The use of juries of verdict was well established by the middle of the thirteenth century, although at first the petty jury also acted upon their own knowledge of the facts. However, in due course witnesses and documentary evidence were being consulted by juries, and by the reign of Henry IV (1399-1413), evidence was being heard in open court.

Over the course of time, the jury was slowly transformed from givers of sworn evidence to being only judges of the evidence of others. By the fifteenth century trial by evidence was established as the norm, and Trevelyan tells us "the jury system, more or less as we now have it, was already the boast of Englishmen, proudly contrasted by Chief Justice Fortescue (served 1442-61) with French procedure, where torture was freely used". By the reign of Mary I (1553-1558) juries were not summoned on account of any supposed or actual knowledge of the facts of a case, but were in fact assumed to be ignorant of the facts until informed of them at trial. Juries were commonly victimized by the Sovereign's court of personal executive power (the "Star Chamber") when the Crown disliked a verdict, and juries were only finally afforded protection from prosecution (for bringing in a wrong verdict) in 1670.

Somewhat later than in England (like, almost six hundred years later), the jury of verdict was introduced by revolutionary France as a symbol of popular emancipation, and was spread widely throughout Europe by Napoleon. However, by the mid-nineteenth century it had waned substantially in the civil law countries. Both the Fascists and the Soviets abolished it completely in their territories, and France did not restore it after the Nazi occupation. Japan abolished the jury system in 1943. In many former British colonies in Africa and Asia, the jury has been replaced by panels of judges or tribunals. Thus the jury has reverted to being essentially an Anglo-Saxon institution, providing a tangible link to England's history every time one is assembled in any of the English speaking countries.

Constitutional Matters Continued . . .

Hubert Walter, Archbishop of Canterbury and regent in the absence of Richard I (1189-99) on the third crusade, granted charters to various towns, allowing them a degree of self-government through elected officials. Similarly, he employed rural gentry in the roles of Justices of the Peace, defending the King's judicial and financial rights in the shires. And in so doing he caused the English middle class to commence learning the habits of conducting public business, and electing representatives.

In the later reigns of John (1199-1216) and Henry III (1216-1272), men started to consider "the law" as having a life of its own, distinct from regal power. In large measure this fact can be attributed to the development of a distinct legal profession in the thirteenth and fourteenth centuries, and to the most famous document in English constitutional history, Magna Carta.

Magna Carta

King John's financial exactions from Barons and Church alike, to finance his failed attempts to win back Normandy from the King of France, were highly injurious, and only success could have saved him from a Baronial backlash. His ultimate failure in 1214 shattered his prestige, and Magna Carta was granted by John in 1215 under threat of civil war, fomented by Stephen Langton, Archbishop of Canterbury. The "Great Charter" differed fundamentally from earlier charters granted by Kings Henry I (1100-1135), Stephen (1135-1154) and Henry II, both because it was much more specific, and because it was extracted from the King, rather than granted by him.

The import of the charter is to circumscribe the powers of the King through the common law and baronial assemblies, and through alliances with other classes. And therein lay the seed of the Barons' success - they were not strong enough alone to rebel against the King without the assistance of other aggrieved parties (other classes, and London) - and since they had the support of these other parties, there was no one for King John to call upon for support. The charter had the actual or tacit support of "the English people" as a whole (or at least, those classes of it which were politically relevant), and may truly be seen as a seminal document in the political development of the English State (and therefore of the United States, and all Commonwealth countries). Protection from the King's officers, and the right to a fair trial by one's peers were granted to all "freemen" - and the importance of that word lies in the fact that over the three hundred years following the signing of Magna Carta the term "freeman" eventually came to mean "everybody". The charter also provided that no extraordinary taxation could be imposed by the Sovereign without such taxation being approved by a council (one might say a parliament) of archbishops, bishops, earls, barons, and so forth. As Trevelyan says: "A process had begun which was to end in putting the power of the Crown into the hands of the community at large".

The next player to take the stage is the immortal Simon de Montfort, who led a popular (rather than just baronial) rebellion against Henry III, attributable ultimately to a general dislike of Henry's tendency to favour foreigners at his court (which is ironic, considering that Simon was himself a Frenchman). Simon's rebellion had the broad support of the middle class of town and country, as well as that of the Barons and Friars. His famous victory over the King at Lewes in 1264 made him the ruler of England for a year (until his defeat and death at Evesham in 1265, at the hands of Henry's magnificent son, the future Edward I). In that brief period, he formalised what had been King Henry III's occasional habit of calling two or more knights from each county to his Parliament, and extended it in a momentous way, by also calling two representatives from each chartered borough (town). Thus the middle class of town and country attended together, for the first time, the institution which was destined to become the supreme legislative assembly of the country. Simon was killed all too soon afterwards, but fortunately Prince Edward had already drawn two important conclusions from Simon's rebellion and initiatives: that the King should reign under the law, and that the Crown was stronger when allied with Parliament, than when opposed to it.

After he became King (1272), Edward extended de Montfort's practice of calling county and borough representatives to his Parliament, with the aims of keeping the Crown in touch with the nation, and the nation in touch with the Crown. Things were put on a formal basis in 1295, when two knights of each shire; two citizens of each city; and two burgesses of each borough were called to a Parliament. Parliaments at this time were still councils dominated by the King and magnates, but the knights and burghers (together known as "the Commons") were able to provide valuable additional information and advice to the King, and feedback to the populace. And an imperceptible transformation thereby took place, because as the Commons slowly became the usual means by which the Sovereign communicated with and extracted taxes from the populace, so these same people gained the power to choke revenues off if they saw fit, and thereby slowly gained influence over the King. Furthermore, after so many years of anarchy and misrule under his father, Edward found much evidence of corruption and abuse of authority amongst royal officers (especially sheriffs), and it was Parliament which became the place where the King or his senior advisers considered petitions from the people, complaining of the misdeeds of these, and other, malefactors.

Context 1250

It might be interesting to pause at three points during this discussion to consider how the constitutional developments then taking place in England compared with those taking place elsewhere, at similar times. We shall use the dates 1250, 1500 and 1750 as rough markers, and remark upon developments in England and in various other countries as close as practicable to those dates.

It should be considcred that rulers everywhere have always needed counsellors, confidantes and cronies around them to execute their orders, manage their finances and administer their justice (or tyranny). These hangers-on often coalesced into councils or "parliaments" (from the French word *parle*: to speak) without those organizations necessarily becoming representative or decision-making institutions in any way. When speaking about parliaments, it is therefore necessary to differentiate between mere talking-shops of the rulers cronies - there to advise the King or assist in the settlement of difficult judicial questions - and institutions which, in however limited a way, were genuinely representative of certain constituencies.

As has been seen, in England an auspicious development took place just after 1250, in that representatives of the boroughs and shires became habitual attendants at "Parliament", although they did not have anything in the way of power at that time. In Scotland, things were less satisfactory, despite the Scottish Crown and the Scottish body-politic having taken on an otherwise Anglo-Norman character by 1250. In the time of de Montfort's English Parliament, the law of Scotland was still entirely feudal, determined by the King. Therefore his Great Council consisted only of nobles and prelates, and his "Parliament" was simply a court of feudal law, staffed by officers and tenants of the King (representatives of the boroughs first attended Scotland's Parliament in 1326). In Ireland, the closest thing to a parliament in 1250 was the English King's Great Council, which was developing along parallel lines to that of its counterpart in England, and was likewise very much still under the English King's thumb.

In France, it was possible for university graduates of non-noble rank to sit in the French "Parlement" by about 1250, but this body merely served as adviser to the King and administrator of his justice, and was in no way representative of the populace. The *Estates General*, on the other hand, which represented the nobles, prelates and bourgeoisie is recorded as having met in 1316 to offer an opinion in the matter of royal succession, but had no power or executive function. The three Estates could never in any case agree between themselves, and this always tended to militate against them gaining power relative to the French monarchs.

Spain was not yet a unified state in 1250, but had largely completed the Reconquest (the Arabs were confined to a small area of southern Spain by that date), and the country was dominated by two major monarchies: Castile-Leon, and Aragon. The fortunes of their respective Parliaments were to follow very different paths, due to the different environments in which they operated. Castile-Leon was for so long cut off from feudal Europe by the Arabs that feudalism never fully developed there. This meant that Castilian kings ruled their subjects directly, rather than through a feudal hierarchy. Thus, the tradition of the monarch needing approval from anyone in particular before taking action was weak in Castile-Leon, and the Castilian Cortes, although theoretically representative of the three estates, never wielded much influence. In Aragon, always more feudal in nature (through closer proximity and more regular intercourse with southern France), the monarchy became fully contractual following a constitutional crisis in 1282, which ended in an excommunicated Aragonese King granting certain constitutional privileges to his nobles and townspeople, in exchange for their renewed allegiance. In any case, some Aragonese nobles held feudal lands independent of the King, and this further tended to militate against absolute regal authority. Thus, the vaguely representative Aragonese Cortes had developed some real authority (although still within the very limited meaning of the term characteristic of the times), and was showing some distinct promise, by about 1250.

In India, the Delhi Sultanate was clearly the most powerful state in northern India by 1250, and was ultimately to hold sway over the whole of the Ganges valley and other parts of northern and central India. By their nature, conquerors are not democrats, and there is no record of representative government either within the sphere of Delhi's hegemony, or outside it, in 1250. Talking of conquerors, in China the Mongols were in power in 1250, with all that the word "Mongol" implies for democracy and freedom of speech! In Japan, the military dictatorship of the Shoguns had recently begun, with the ascendancy of the Kamakura clan (1185-1333). Japan was to remain in a state of feudal anarchy, with no hint of even rudimentary democracy, until after the Meiji Restoration in 1868.

Constitutional Matters Continued...

Back in England, as the fourteenth and fifteenth centuries progressed, so the power of Parliament ebbed and flowed with the political and financial strength of the various monarchs. Almost as a sub-plot, the knights and burghers themselves ("the Commons") became recognized as a legitimate component of Parliament, and began to originate complaints and requests for redress. By the reign of Henry VI (1422-61, 1470-71), the more important of these actions were taking the form of "bills", to be debated upon and passed into law by Parliament as a whole. The Commons' prestige and influence also gradually increased throughout the fourteenth and fifteenth centuries because, being neither allied to the Crown nor to the nobles, they ended up becoming a "third force", holding the balance of power in the constant war and/or quarrelling between the Crown and Barons during that period.

And so it was that in the one hundred and fifty years following Edward I's accession in 1272 the House of Commons (which started life as informal meetings of the knights and burghers alone, to determine their collective response to some matter being discussed by Parliament as a whole) gained an important place in England's constitution. The strongest forces remained the Crown, Barons and Church, but the Commons became an intrinsic part of the machinery of government, and became originators of or indispensable parties to, all new laws, extraordinary taxation, and even *coups d'etat*.

Context - 1500

We should not fool ourselves that the foregoing means that the representatives of the shires and boroughs yet had much power. Whilst it is true that, by 1500, English monarchs required the agreement of the Lords and Commons for any new law or taxation, there was in fact little need for any new laws or taxes (the personal estates of the monarchs provided sufficient revenues for most ordinary purposes). Therefore, the Commons had little effective power at this date. Nevertheless, in the matter of genuine representation of (some of) the people, England appears to be unique, in that its parliament developed into a genuinely representative institution (if not a seat of executive power) during the thirteenth to sixteenth centuries - that is to say, it developed into an institution where the "common people" would at least be heard, and might affect outcomes. "Parliaments" were developing across Europe at the same time as in England, but they were not representative institutions in this sense.

The development of more expensive weaponry, which caused an increase in the costs of waging war or keeping the peace, was at this time tending to increase the power of monarchs throughout Europe vis-à-vis their nobles. The Renaissance was also disseminating knowledge of Roman law widely, which encouraged the view that the will of the Sovereign was law. Thus, in most of Europe (and in Scotland) royal government was tending towards absolutism throughout the period. In England, however, the malleable, pragmatic and resilient common law, and the decisive alliance which had formed between the wealthy and conservative legal profession and the Commons in Parliament proved equal to the task, and did not allow the English monarchs to go the way of their counterparts elsewhere.

At the turn of the sixteenth century Scotland's Parliament remained entirely feudal in form, acting as little more than a court of registration, recording the law as laid down by the absolutist monarch. Thus Chrimes (see bibliography) was able to note that James VI of Scotland (1567-1625) was brought up in a constitutional environment entirely alien to that which he found when he became James I of England (1603-1625) - this despite the existence, by his day, of the General Assembly of the (Presbyterian) Church, which was a quasi-democratic institution. In English-ruled Ireland, as was the case in 1250, the word "parliament" has no representative meaning in 1500.

In France, the promise that the Estates General had shown in the fourteenth century was not realised, since France remained a feudal country, and was to move in the seventeenth century to the full absolutism of Louis XIV. Under the financial stress of the Hundred Years' War, the direct taxes which the French kings had long since extracted from their own peasants (on their own royal lands) were extended nationally, and in the latter stages of the war they were made permanent. Therefore, the French kings were always able to get by without the Estates-General, which were only rarely called, in times of crisis. On the rare occasions that the Estates General did meet, they were simply called by kings who required a rubber stamp for an intended course of action, and were not allowed to become "representative" in any proper sense of the word.

In Castile-Leon an equivalent of the French direct tax, uncontrolled by the Cortes, had been levied since the fourteenth century, and this had made the Castilian Cortes dispensable. In Aragon, the Cortes retained control of revenues and therefore remained more relevant and vaguely representative. However, when Spain was "unified" in 1479, the more authoritarian Castilian model prevailed (in no small measure through the efforts of the Inquisition), and the "Catholic Kings" Ferdinand of Aragon and Isabella of Castile ruled as absolutist monarchs. By the reign of their grandson Charles V (1516-1556), the King's executive orders were being carried out or audited by the Inquisition, and Spain was becoming the model and inspiration for the many other absolutist European states which would develop in the following century and a half.

India was politically and religiously fragmented in 1500, and the rajas, sultans and other potentates who each ran their own states were not well known for their democratic inclinations. Nor did the establishment of the Moghul empire in 1526 do anything to promote democracy in India. In China, the year 1500 marks approximately the middle of the Ming period (1368-1644), the latest in a long line of autocratic Chinese dynasties with no sympathy for the democratic principle. Japan was a mess in 1500, with no clear national leader and the great military clans engaged in almost constant civil war. Needless to say, such conditions meant that democracy still did not exist there either.

Constitutional Matters Continued - Tudor England

The Wars of the Roses exterminated most male members of the great families which traditionally provided opposition to the English Crown. Henry VII extinguished what little feudal opposition remained, by purging his Privy Council of nobles and replacing them with obedient bureaucrats. He was thus able to hand on to his son a powerful and undisputed Crown, and a full exchequer.

In certain respects the two greatest Tudors, Henry VIII and Elizabeth I, were despotic in temperament and behaviour, and yet it seemed natural to both of them that they were not above the law, and that the law was something more than just their will. It was also clear to them that allied *with* the law, English monarchs were becoming a formidable force: Trevelyan tells us that by the time of Henry VIII's accession in 1509, "the nation could do nothing against the will of the Crown, and the Crown nothing against the will of the nation, but the two together could do anything they chose".

Parliament's prestige had taken a step backwards during the Wars of the Roses (since issues were generally decided at the point of the sword during this period), but was increased considerably by its role in the extremely difficult matter of Henry VIII's struggle with Rome. The legislation which completed the breach with Rome (1534) was passed after discussion by both Houses, and during this decisive period Parliament sat for seven years, and built up a strong continuity of experience. In 1543 the Commons was granted the important right of immunity from arrest during session. Henry also encouraged freedom of speech within the House for his own diplomatic purposes (he was thus able to tell the Pope that his Parliament supported him freely in all that he was doing).

The most important constitutional developments arising from the Reformation were that papal authority was abolished in England, and the legislative powers of the Clergy were subordinated to the Crown and Parliament. Royal supremacy over the Church in England was recognized and legitimized by Act of Parliament.

The fundamental constitutional question remained, however - was the Sovereign or Parliament destined to be supreme? The inevitable show-down was deferred during the Tudor period, in part due to the forcefulness of the personalities of Henry VIII and Elizabeth, and in part due to the unifying effects of various political events which occurred during their reigns.

Stuart England

Thus, resolution of the awkward constitutional questions which remained was held over until the coming of less adroit and less admired monarchs: the Stuarts. It was during their monarchy that the question of whether the Crown or Parliament ruled the country was, indeed, effectively decided. The transformation was effected in three stages; firstly, the lower House turned itself into a real opposition; then into a body capable of effective government (through the development of an elaborate committee system), and ultimately into an actual government.

The Petition of Right

The Stuarts were men of their times, with an inclination to despotism and arbitrary power. They legislated by proclamation; they gave selective dispensations from the law; and they granted a burgeoning jurisdiction to their prerogative courts. The first constitutional landmark of the period arises after the country had enjoyed twenty five years of this brand of monarchy, with the Petition of Right (1628).

The Petition of Right listed various ancient statutes which had been supposed to assure the rights of the King's subjects, reported a litany of recent abuses of those rights, and "humbly prayed" that:

> no man should be compelled to yield any tax without the agreement of Parliament;

> no man should be imprisoned or detained against the form of Magna Carta or the law;

> soldiers and marines should not be billeted upon private persons; and

> martial law should not be brought to bear upon the general populace.

A Petition of Right does not change the law, but by giving his assent to the Petition, Charles I made a serious moral concession to Parliament.

Another development from about this time concerns freedom of speech within Parliament. Freedom of speech had always been claimed as a right of Parliament (and as has just been seen, was encouraged by Tudor monarchs who had little to fear from Parliament), but the question was finally settled in the case of the Crown versus Sir John Elliot and others in 1629. The gentlemen in question were convicted of having made seditious speeches within Parliament, but both Houses of Parliament declared that judgment to be illegal. In 1688, the right to freedom of speech within Parliament was enshrined in the Bill of Rights, and has not been questioned since.

As has been seen in chapter 1, Charles I dispensed with Parliament in 1629, and became increasingly authoritarian in style. The Scottish Rebellion of 1638-40 eventually compelled Charles to recall Parliament, so that money could be voted to finance a response. Unfortunately for the royal power, Parliament insisted upon settling constitutional matters first, and as a result of their efforts at this moment, all possibility of lawful supremacy of King over Parliament was forever extinguished. This was achieved through various Acts which laid down that Parliaments would meet regularly, and could not be dissolved by the monarch within forty days of their assembly, without their consent. In addition, all arbitrary authority of the King was abolished, through the sweeping away of various of his prerogative courts. The best known of these was the Court of Star Chamber (named for the decorations in the room often used for its meetings), which had been in existence since about 1348, and was the organ of the King's personal jurisdiction in criminal matters. It developed an appalling reputation for severe sentences, arbitrary decisions, and secrecy, and its abolition in 1641 was lamented by none but the most rabid of royalists.

The principle of Parliamentary supremacy was in due course taken to extremes, as Charles was executed and the country and empire were ruled directly by the House of Commons until 1660. By the time Charles II was called upon by Parliament to take up the Crown, it was no longer possible for a monarch to govern England without the participation of the House of Commons; from this time the King, Lords, Commons and the courts of common law each clearly had their own rights, and were each indispensable components of the government. Charles II's treacherous acceptance of financial assistance from Louis XIV during the last few years of his life could not alter this fact, but only circumvent it for a short while.

When the country had finally had enough of the Stuarts in 1688, the last of their line (the bigoted and deluded James II) was thrown out and the Crown was passed to William III and Mary *by Parliament.* Parliament became, in effect, the sovereign legislative authority, and true constitutional or contractual monarchy began. The instrument of this change was the Bill of Rights, which vested the Crown in William and Mary (James II being deemed to have abdicated), defined the succession after those monarchs, and excluded Catholics from the possibility of succession.

This bill commenced by listing the many crimes of James II, and then declared (amongst other things) that:

the suspension or execution of laws without the consent of Parliament is illegal;

levying money for the use of the Crown by royal prerogative is illegal;

legislation designed to prevent subjects petitioning the King is illegal;

the raising of a standing army without the consent of Parliament is illegal;

freedom of speech within Parliament is sacrosanct;

Parliaments ought to be held frequently.

The "Glorious Revolution" of 1688 ousted a lawful monarch, and made it abundantly clear that kings of England were thereafter kings by Act of Parliament, and that when push came to shove, Parliament was supreme over the Crown. The rights and authorities of the Crown, Lords, Commons and the courts of common law were clarified, and each had their respective place in the scheme of things confirmed. The almost complete independence of each of these four pillars of the constitution within their proper spheres of authority came to be widely admired abroad, including in the American colonies (the arrangement was later replicated, as best as possible, by the authors of the American Constitution).

The fourth and final landmark in English constitutional history came soon after, in 1701.

The Act of Settlement

By 1700, Mary was dead, William III was ailing, and Mary's sister Anne appeared to be past the age of childbirth (having had seventeen children already, none of whom had survived her). Thus, it became urgently necessary to establish the succession after Anne, who would herself be raised to the throne upon William's death (which occurred in 1702).

The succession was vested in the House of Hanover, but this is of less significance here than the provisions embodied in the Act of Settlement, that (amongst other things):

> any person inheriting the Crown should subscribe to the Bill of Rights;

> judges could not be removed by the Crown; and

> any impeachment by Parliament may not be overturned by the Crown.

Incidentally, impeachment is a topical issue, because at the time of writing the impeachment trial of U.S. President Bill Clinton is still a recent memory. The verdict in Clinton's impeachment was never in doubt, and is irrelevant here; what is notable is the parallels between the US impeachment process and the ancient English process whence it comes. In England, impeachment came into use during the last years of the reign of Edward III (1327-1377), and is the means by which Parliament brings members of the executive to book for misdemeanours. Impeachment is the prosecution of an offender by the Commons (for which, read the U.S. House of Representatives) before the Lords (for which, read the U.S. Senate). The Lords act as judges, and pronounce the accused guilty or not guilty, but cannot pass judgment unless the Commons demand it.

It can be seen that the period 1628-1701 was of the utmost importance from a constitutional point of view. During that period the rivalry of Crown and Parliament was finally brought to a head, and the issue was forever decided in favour of the latter. A cooperative relationship between the two was substituted thereafter, and the political and personal freedoms of the individual were substantially advanced (albeit still only to be enjoyed by a small proportion of the population), and the right of English kings to rule was firmly shown to be in the hands of Parliament. During this period, the Star Chamber was abolished, judges ceased to be removable at the will of the Crown, and the even balance of the powerful Whig and Tory parties protected critics of government who spoke from either camp.

The Cabinet System

An identifiable forerunner of the modern Cabinet system was the small group of advisers (called the "Cabal") which Charles II developed the habit of consulting. The Cabal was uncontrolled by the later conventions of the Cabinet system, and did not allow for responsibility to be pinned onto known individuals, because of its secretive nature.

Over the course of the eighteenth century a Cabinet system proper developed, as did the office of Prime Minister, and the ministry system (departments ultimately answerable to Parliament which conducted the increasingly complex business of the State). It was through these three "inventions" that England (Britain) was able to conduct efficient government by a small and united executive ultimately responsible to Parliament. This system has since been adopted by many countries (not only former dominions and colonies) and stands, in the opinion of Trevelyan, as "England's chief contribution to the science of political mechanism". Not that the system was perfected until the nineteenth century: in 1801 an incoming Prime Minister had to point out to an out-going Lord Chancellor that his attendance at Cabinet meetings was no longer required!

By the time of the Napoleonic Wars the Cabinet system was nevertheless well developed, and those wars were fought by a quick-footed Cabinet constrained only by a requirement to explain its intentions and strategy to the Commons periodically.

During the reign of George III (1760-1820) it became the custom to publish the names of Cabinet members, and for the Prime Minister to nominate his own colleagues within Cabinet. In 1841, the convention that the Cabinet may only sit with the support of a majority in the House was established.

Context 1750

In eighteenth century Britain (that is, England, Scotland and Wales), the Commons remained very unrepresentative, and the wheels of government were kept turning by widespread bribery and corruption of politicians by the Crown. The only good things which can be said about this is that deadlock arising from disputes between the immovable object of the Crown and the irresistible force of Parliament were thereby prevented, and that it allowed for the rise of some young men who turned out to be extremely able politicians and statesmen, through the patronage of mentors. As Chrimes astutely puts it: "A genuine aristocracy always tends to patronize ability, whereas democracy usually tends to patronize mediocrity, for it understands that better".

Nevertheless, there was at least representation of sorts, and the royal power had to a very considerable extent been brought under the control of "the people". A genuine opposition to George III formed in the 1770s, which would take things to their natural conclusion in the following century, reforming the political process in such a way as to ultimately remove the Crown from the sphere of politics altogether. Nevertheless, it was not until the twentieth century, during the reign of Edward VII (1901-10) that an English Sovereign first explicitly stated that "the King never expresses an opinion on political matters except on the advice of his responsible ministers".

In 1720 the Irish Parliament had been officially proclaimed subordinate to the English government, represented in Ireland by the viceroy in Dublin Castle. Furthermore, pursuant to an Act of 1729, it was hardly representative of the broad Irish populace in any case, since the right of Catholics to vote (about 75 per cent of the population) had been abolished. Those people whom it did "represent" - Protestants - were as poorly served as their counterparts in England, for the same reasons: "rotten boroughs", bribery and the like.

During the sixteenth and seventeenth centuries, the ability of kings to tax their subjects was granting European monarchs a monopoly over the new and expensive weapons of war, and this led to the rise of absolute monarchy. Almost everywhere, the authority of European rulers advanced at the expense of their competitors: "over-mighty nobles", and representative bodies.

In France in 1750, Louis XV was doing a fine job of emulating that European absolutist *par excellence*, his great-grandfather Louis XIV. Parlement remained an elitist, self-serving and largely ineffective institution, and the Estates General, which ostensibly represented nobles, clergy and commoners, was not called between the dates 1614 and 1788, by which time Louis XV was dead, and France was heading for revolution. The authority and jurisdiction of this very imperfect body had become so uncertain by 1788 (through long desuetude) that it could then achieve very little to slow the descent into chaos. As an aside, many of the changes which the French Revolution wrought in France and Europe had already existed in England for centuries - such as representative parliaments (albeit imperfect) and the jury system. The English middle-class had a share of power long before that of other European countries, which might in part explain why there was no revolution in England in the dangerous 1830s and 40s, when the rest of Europe was in ferment.

In Spain, the War of the Spanish Succession (1701-13) had placed Bourbon kings on the Spanish throne who shared their French relatives' aversion to democracy. The war had turned what was effectively a federation of Spanish states into a more or less unitary state within the modern Spanish borders, and had brought the whole country under direct royal administration. By about 1750, the Spanish monarchs had also introduced certain French administrative practices which strengthened royal control over local administrations. Thus, the Spanish State remained absolutist in temperament, and the words "representation of the people" still had little meaning.

An indication of how things were going in some other European states in 1750 is provided by an examination of serfdom, since any State which will countenance serfdom is, by definition, an undemocratic one. Essentially, anyone who found themselves in this nasty and supremely disenfranchised position differed from a slave only insofar as a serf was a chattel attached to land, whereas a slave was generally sold "unencumbered". Serfdom was not abolished in most of the Austro-Hungarian empire until 1781 (in Hungary not until a little later); not until 1806 in the Confederation of the Rhine (successor to the Holy Roman Empire); and not until 1861 in Russia.

The United States can now be mentioned. The democratic principles enshrined in the American constitution (1788) cause that document to be widely admired as a landmark in world history, and it has ever since inspired liberals and revolutionaries everywhere - not least in France in 1789. In designing their system of government, the colonials took the best constitution that they could find (the British one) and modified it as befitted their local circumstances and their anti-monarchical views. Thus they determined that the country should be run by a "monarch" (albeit elected, in the American case) at the head of an executive government (Cabinet), kept in check by a bicameral legislature - the Senate (Lords) and the House of Representatives (Commons).

In India, the Moghul empire had disintegrated into a gaggle of autonomous states by 1750, and these were to be superseded eventually by the equally undemocratic British East India Company. Thus, representative democracy was still unknown to that land. Similarly in Ch'ing dynasty China (1644-1912) there was no possibility of representation of the people. In 1750, Japan was enjoying its "great peace" under the Tokugawa Shogunate (1603-1867), another feudal dictatorship under which there was no possibility of democratic representation.

Thus, even by 1750 democratic institutions had not really developed or survived anywhere else of note, whilst they had already long been part of England's constitutional landscape.

Constitutional Matters Continued - Nineteenth and Twentieth Century Reform

Reform was seriously considered towards the end of the eighteenth century, but a reaction to the French Revolution, and the widespread feeling during the Napoleonic Wars that strong government was probably more important than representative government at that moment, delayed matters until after the storm had passed. Some highlights of the general movement towards Parliamentary reform that have characterized the last two centuries are the Reform Acts of 1832, 1867, 1884-5 and 1918, and the introduction of the secret ballot in 1873. At the end of the process, the modern system of executive government by a Cabinet answerable to a genuinely representative Parliament was effectively in place.

The Reform Act of 1832 broadened the franchise (which had been unchanged since 1430) to now include many smaller property owners, and redistributed representation from the "rotten boroughs" controlled by landowners, to the rapidly growing industrial centres. Indeed it went further than that in a moral sense, because it became clear that a trend had been established towards an ever widening franchise, and this caused politicians to start taking into account not only the views of the current electorate, but those of the likely future electorate. Needless to say, the proposal was unpopular in the House of Lords, and was only passed at a third attempt in face of a threat to create sufficient new Liberal peers to ensure its passage. The Reform Act of 1867 further broadened the franchise to many working men in the towns and cities, and the Act of 1884 broadened it further still to agricultural workers and miners, whilst the Redistribution Act of 1885 set representation at one member per 50,000 of population. By Acts of Parliament dated 1911 and 1949, the House of Lords' ancient power of veto was removed, and substituted with a power of short delay for most bills (but no delay for money bills). Almost full male suffrage, and limited female suffrage was granted in 1918 in Britain (one of her colonies, New Zealand, had been the first country in the world to grant female suffrage in national elections, in 1893), and unqualified female suffrage in Britain was introduced in 1928.

Conclusion

The fifteen hundred years of English constitutional history which have been the subject of this chapter have profoundly affected many nations around the world, most notably Scotland, Wales, Ireland, the United States of America, and the Commonwealth nations. England's constitutional arrangements set her apart from all other nations, and deserve to stand very highly in the esteem of those people who live under them, or under one of their derivatives. The jury system has receded in the non-English-speaking countries and in South Africa, but England's common law remains, sometimes synthesized with religious laws (e.g. India, Malaysia), and sometimes synthesized with native customs (e.g. Africa and Oceania). English common law has developed a monstrous life of its own in the United States, and has been merged with civil law (derived from Roman law) in such places as Scotland, the Philippines, Quebec (Canada), Louisiana (USA) and South Africa. The forms of England's parliamentary democracy (if not the realities, in some cases) also survive in many countries spread all around the world.

These three things - trial by jury, English common law, and England's parliamentary system - are woven intricately into the stuff of over one and a half billion lives, worldwide, and stand very much to the eternal credit of the English nation.

Chapter 4

THE ENGLISH LANGUAGE

The English language has effectively become "the world's language". It is spoken as a mother tongue by around four hundred million people, and the total number of English speakers (including fluent speakers of it as a foreign language, and Pidgin English speakers) probably exceeds one billion, surpassed only in numbers (but not geographic distribution) by the various Chinese dialects. Three-quarters of the world's electronic communication is in English, and more than eighty per cent of the data stored in the world's computers is in English.

English is an exceptionally rich and deep language; the largest English dictionaries list around four hundred thousand English words, whereas the French and German languages, for example, have vocabularies of less than half that size.

Origins

Old (Anglo-Saxon) English was a Germanic language, but Modern English can be very roughly described as half Germanic and half Romance (French and Latin), with a liberal smattering of Greek and other European languages.

At the time of the Conquest, there were four predominant Old English dialects, being Northumbrian (from which the Scots dialect derives), Mercian, West Saxon and Kentish. It is one of the Mercian sub-dialects, East Midland, which is the ancestor of the world's "Modern English", through having been spoken in

London, Oxford and Cambridge, and through having been the language of Chaucer and Wycliffe.

However, to retrace our steps for a moment, English (in its various forms) remained the language of the indigenous population following the Conquest (although it drew heavily from northern French dialects), while the Normans stuck at first to their own tongue. This was fortuitous, because it meant that English could adapt itself quietly to the changing needs of its native speakers over the course of about three hundred years, without interference from the clergy (who spoke Latin) or the gentry (who spoke French).

By the middle of the fourteenth century, things had changed. In 1362 a law was passed through Parliament stating that since the French language was by then "much unknown in this realm", all pleadings (in courts of law) should in future be spoken in English. The first written record of a parliamentary debate in English dates from this same year, and the first known property deed, and the first will written in English date from just a few years later. This switch to English in the second half of the fourteenth century can be attributed to a number of things: firstly, the Hundred Years' War (which caused French to become the language of the enemy again); secondly, the increasing participation by native English speakers in Parliament; and thirdly, the lead given by the Crown and nobles (for example, Henry IV was careful to address Parliament in English in 1399 after he had deposed Richard II).

The East Midland dialect had become the de facto English language by Tudor times, and was disseminated nationwide via the English Bible (which Henry VIII ordered should be placed in every parish church) and the Prayer Book, fixing it firmly as the standard.

Thus, by the time of the first English plantations abroad, English more or less as it is currently spoken was the established language of the land (although it was not until the eighteenth century that academics ceased writing in Latin, and adopted English instead).

English as a first or second language

The English language is spoken on a regular basis in more than sixty countries around the world, on every inhabited continent.

At the end of the sixteenth century, just before the first successful foreign settlement by the English (excepting Ireland), it is estimated that about five to seven million people spoke the English language (almost all of whom, of course, resided in Britain). At the present day, English is the first language for around three hundred and eighty to four hundred million people around the world, most of whom do not live in Britain.

In the United States, where the majority of all "mother-tongue" English speakers reside, English is not actually "established" or sanctioned as the official language of the State. English is, however, the sole official language in England, Scotland, Australia, the former British colonies in the West Indies, and most of the former British colonies in Black Africa.

English is a second language (i.e. not the mother tongue) for about three hundred to four hundred million more people. It should be noted that this figure is highly subjective, and is affected heavily by the estimations made for such populous countries as Nigeria and India.

English shares official status with other languages in Wales, Ireland, Canada, New Zealand, India, South Africa, Malaysia, Hong Kong, The Philippines, Singapore and Tanzania.

English as the world's Lingua Franca

Lingua Franca (literally, the language of the Franks) is a Latin phrase which has come to mean "a common language". The Frankish language once played this role in north-western Europe, but English now performs it worldwide. Apart from the possibly eight hundred million people already mentioned as speakers of English as a first or second language, it is estimated that a further one hundred million people speak English *fluently* as a foreign language. If "broken English" speakers are added to this figure, several hundred million more people would come within the clutches of the English language (figures are affected heavily by any estimations made for India and China).

British colonial and imperial activity from the seventeenth century onwards, and Britain's power and prestige in the eighteenth and nineteenth centuries, commenced the process of disseminating the English language worldwide. However, due credit must be given to the twentieth century British and American music industries, and the American film industry (much as linguistic purists would be horrified to admit it), since it is these media which now seem to be completing the task of worldwide dissemination.

English is now the predominant language of international business, international tourism, science, technology, sport, diplomacy and academic activity. It is the language of international air traffic control, and is becoming the standard language of international maritime affairs, policing, and emergency operations. Thus, many people the world over now find it essential to learn English as a necessary medium of their education or profession, and virtually everybody is now using it as the common language of communication where a *lingua franca* is required.

English can also serve a convenient political role in some countries. This is most notably the case in India (population approx. one billion), where the issue of which language to speak can be a political one, sometimes best solved by the use of English as a "neutral" third language.

Some countries (most notably France) are currently attempting to restrain the ever-widening influence of the English language upon their own tongues, but it is to be presumed that they will have limited success in the long run, other than at an official level. An amusing piece concerning the pointless and hopeless efforts of the *Acadamie Francais* to keep the French language "pure", in order to ensure that it does not die, should be quoted. Claiborne (see bibliography) says:

> "The truth is that if borrowing foreign words could destroy a language, English would be dead (borrowed from Old Norse), deceased (from French), defunct (from Latin) and kaput (from German). When it comes to borrowing, English excels (from Latin), surpasses (from French) and eclipses (from Greek) any other tongue, past or present".

Significance

The significance of the fact that the "Anglo-American" nations (most notably the United Kingdom and the United States) speak English is difficult to judge, but is probably immense. Certainly it is not fanciful to suppose that the sympathy and active assistance provided by the United States to Britain and her other allies in two twentieth century wars were in no small measure ultimately attributable to this fact.

Furthermore, the fact that the language of the only remaining superpower is English is probably also of enormous significance to America's fellow English-speaking nations. There tends to be a natural affinity amongst people who speak the same language, and this probably manifests itself in a thousand inscrutable ways in the diplomatic arena. Similarly, when businesses in English-speaking countries are choosing locations for branch offices, there is an obvious tendency to see other English-speaking countries as logical first choices (all other things being equal). This would not matter much if it were not for the fact that two of these English-speaking countries, namely America and Britain, are very large and economically significant.

Footnote

The English language has always been very open to outside influence, and is not only rich with French, Latin and Greek words and phrases such as *joie de vivre*, *lingua franca*, and *kaleidoscope*, but also with other European words and phrases such as *peccadillo* (Spanish), *realpolitik* (German), *stanza* (Italian), and *sputnik* (Russian).

It has also been enriched by many words and phrases derived from England's naval, military and general history, or picked up along the way from various parts of Britain's empire. A sample follows:

From the Royal Navy

Blazer (smart vertically-striped jacket). Such a garment was supplied by a Commanding Officer of *HMS Blazer* to his boats-crew in 1845, and is still standard dress at the Henley Rowing Regatta;

Cold enough to freeze the balls off a brass monkey (extremely cold). Brass monkeys were storage tracks for cannon balls, mounted alongside cannon on the old warships. Allegedly, in extreme cold the iron cannon balls could contract sufficiently to slip through the brass tracks, and fall. It should be noted that this is highly doubtful from a physical point of view: therefore the expression has probably always been figurative rather than literal;

Copper-bottomed (safe or guaranteed). Derived from the copper sheathing which was applied to wooden hulls, to protect them from attack by Teredo worms;

First rate, second rate, etc. (warships were rated by size and armament, with a ship of the first rate having the most decks, and carrying the most guns);

Force four, etc. (a reference to the Beaufort scale of wind velocity, devised by Admiral Sir Francis Beaufort RN, in 1805);

Half-Nelson (a reference to Lord Nelson, whose arm was shot away during an amphibious assault on Tenerife);

Navy Blue (a dark shade of blue used in, and popularized by, the uniform of the British Royal Navy);

Nipper (small boy). Derived from the short pieces of rope used by ship's boys to "nip" [or temporarily attach] an anchor cable to an endless loop of rope being rolled around capstans, when raising an anchor;

Piping hot (extremely hot). Derived from the fact that when a meal had been prepared on board, the crew were notified that it was ready by means of the bosun's pipe;

Show a leg ("wake up"). Derived from the fact that females, when they were allowed to stay onboard warships, were allowed to linger in their hammocks after the crew had been called to their duties. As the bosun did his rounds, females could identify themselves by poking their leg out of their hammock for inspection;

Sling your hook (get lost). As in: "sling the hooks of your hammock somewhere else, please";

Toe the line (obey the rules). Derived from the custom in the old days of calling each man forward to a line marked on the deck, so that he might identify himself and receive his pay or rations;

True colours (true nature or character). Derived from the tradition of always hoisting one's true flag of nationality before engaging the enemy, even if one had approached in disguise - i.e. flying false colours;

Turn a blind eye (ignore an indiscretion etc.). Derived from Lord Nelson's famous ploy of putting his telescope to his blind eye when he wished to ignore the "Withdraw" signal hoisted by his Commander-in-Chief at the Battle of Copenhagen.

From the British Army

Balaclava (woollen hood for head and shoulders). Such headgear was knitted for and worn by British troops at the Battle of Balaclava during the Crimean War;

Tank (when the armoured vehicle which the English-speaking world calls a tank was being developed during the First World War, the British Army put it about, for security reasons, that what was being developed was a vehicle which could transport water across battle fields - in other words, a mobile water *tank*. The code-name stuck);

To meet one's Waterloo (Napoleon's final battle in 1815, after which he was exiled to St. Helena);

From Other Sources

Banshee (spirit whose wail portends death in a house). From Irish *bean sidhe*;

Black hole of Calcutta (hell-hole or claustrophobic space). A reference to the room designed to hold three men in which an Indian Potentate incarcerated between sixty four and one hundred and forty six British prisoners in 1756. Only about twenty two prisoners survived the night;

Bloody Mary (vodka and tomato juice). From the epithet for Mary I (1553-1558), so named because of her persecution of Protestants;

Bobby (policeman). From the nickname "Bobby's Boys" given to Sir Robert Peel's Metropolitan Police, set up under his Metropolitan Police Act of 1829;

Boxing day (uniquely English name for the day after Christmas). Derived from the practice of the English Church distributing boxes at Christmas into which unwanted toys and other gifts could be placed for the poor;

Boycott (sever from communication). From Charles Cunningham Boycott, a retired British Army Officer who managed some estates in Ireland for an absentee landlord. He refused to lower rents in response to poor economic conditions in 1880, and was "boycotted";

Cabal (secretive political clique). From the initials of five advisers to Charles II - Lord Clifford, Lord Arlington, the Duke of Buckingham, Lord Ashley and Lord Lauderdale);

Calico (cheap cotton cloth). Named after the town of Calicut in India, whence enormous quantities of this fabric originally came;

Char (tea). From the Chinese word *Cha*;

Cheddar (generic name for a type of hard, light orange-yellow, cow's-milk cheese). Named after the cheese manufactured in the Cheddar Gorge, Somerset, since the twelfth century;

Churchillian (tenacious, pugnacious, indomitable). A reference to Sir Winston Churchill;

Dhobi (clothes to be washed, or a washer-woman). *Hindi*;

Dragoon (force into a course of action). From the use to which these cavalrymen have occasionally been put by the authorities;

Dunce (one slow at learning). Derived from the name of Duns Scotus [c 1266-1308], Scottish philosopher and Catholic theologian. Scotus was, in fact, a very intelligent man, but his theories of papal supremacy were naturally unpopular in Reformation England, and so his name was corrupted to "dunce" and the insult was thereafter applied to anybody "unenlightened";

Fellah (bloke). From Arabic for Egyptian peasant;

Jingoism (chauvinism, belligerent nationalism). From the use of the words "by jingo!" in a bellicose song which became popular in England in 1877-78, during the Turko-Russian war;

Juggernaut (massive vehicle). *Krishna* in Hindi, whose idol was dragged in an annual procession upon a giant carriage;

Khaki (dust-coloured or dull yellow). *Hindi*;

Kingmaker (one who procures power for kings, politicians, etc., through his personal influence). A reference to the Earl of Warwick's abilities and activities during the Wars of the Roses;

Limerick (short, humorous verse, in format *aabba*). The origin of the word is uncertain, but may derive from an eighteenth century Irish soldiers' song "Will you come up to Limerick" [Ireland], sung in the metric form 8/8/5/5/8;

Luddite (one who wishes to obstruct progress). From the name of the bands of English artisans who destroyed machinery during the period 1811-16, fearing for their jobs;

"Manchester" (a word used uniquely in New Zealand to mean bed linen and toweling). A reference to the city whence most of New Zealand's bed linen and toweling came in colonial days;

Mufti (plain clothes worn by one entitled to wear uniform). From Arabic for Muslim priest or authority on law;

Namby-pamby (insipid, sentimental, lacking vigour). Derived from the name of Ambrose Philips, an eighteenth century English pastoral writer, whose style was presumably insipid [the present author cannot claim to have read much of Philips' work, so cannot confirm or deny]!;

Newton (a measure of physical force, being that force which, if applied to a free body with a mass of 1 kg., would accelerate that body at the rate of 1 metre per second per second). Named in honour of Sir Isaac Newton;

"Not my cup of tea" (not favoured or preferred). A reference to the myriad blends of this beverage available. Chinese in origin,

tea was first sold publicly in England in 1657;

Prime Minister. Originally a derogatory epithet applied to any member of Charles II's inner circle of ministers who gained especial influence with the King for a while, and might dare to think of himself as the King's "prime" minister. Still a term of derision in the time of Walpole [in power 1721-42, and generally considered to be Britain's first Prime Minister], since the term was only applied to him by his enemies, and was repudiated by Walpole himself;

Pundit (expert or informed commentator). A learned Hindu: *Hindi*;

Rolls-Royce (the best and most luxurious). A reference to the famous marque of motor car;

Sandwich (reputedly named after the 4th Earl of Sandwich, whose chef developed this convenient form of meal, so that his employer need not leave the gaming tables in order to refuel);

Shipshape and Bristol fashion (neat and tidy). Derived from a reputation for seamanlike appearance which was enjoyed by ships trading out of Bristol in the old days;

Star Chamber (arbitrary or oppressive tribunal). A reference to the Court of Star Chamber abolished by the English Parliament in 1641;

Taboo (prohibited, consecrated). *Tongan*;

Thug (cut-throat or ruffian). From Hindu band of assassins called Thuggees, suppressed around 1825;

Utopian (seemingly perfect state of affairs, impossibly idealistic). From the title of Sir Thomas More's book *Utopia* [1516], being the name of his imaginary island state, which derives from the Greek words for *not* [ou] and *place* [topos], i.e. *nowhere*;

Westminster system (referring to the style of parliamentary democracy developed by the English, and operated at the Palace of Westminster and elsewhere);

Whirling Dervish (frenetic or hyper-active person). From the order of Moslem holy men whose practice it was to spin rapidly, to induce an hypnotic state;

Yob (lout or hooligan). Cockney reverse slang for "boy".

Commentary

The significance of such words and phrases as these, in the context of this book, is that they are to be found in widespread usage all around the world. Hundreds of millions of people, from India to the United States of America and from South Africa to New Zealand, will today speak the language of a tiny country which they may never have seen, and may have no interest in. In fact, they may hardly give England a second thought from one year to the next - and yet how do these words and phrases come to be part of their vocabulary? Indeed, how does English come to be the very language which they speak?

Because England made it so, and thereby wove her story into the stuff of a billion lives (and counting).

Chapter 5

THE ENGLISH CONTRIBUTION TO SPORT

Introduction

England's contribution to the development and regulation of international sports has been immense: she has invented several of the best loved sports, and has laid down the accepted rules of many others. England's influence extends into sports that are not even played by the English. For example, of the three major team sports in the United States, only basketball is unequivocally American in origin; the other two (American football and baseball) have clear English ancestry.

English sport has its fair share of fanatical supporters - in particular, the generally admirable "Barmy Army" which follows the English cricket team around the world, and the generally execrable English soccer fans. But England is not unique - or even exceptional - in this regard: there are nations around which can boast even more fanatical sports fans than the English. The Indian sub-continent can come to a standstill when there is an important cricket match on; the entire Welsh and New Zealand nations seem personally affronted when they lose at rugby (the one more often than the other!); and South American soccer fans can be driven to murder and mayhem when they lose an important soccer match.

What *is* unique to England is the pivotal role played by England in the development of these and many other sports, and it may be that it is this feeling of "ownership" of some sports which can explain the outrage and gnashing of teeth in the English press whenever England loses at cricket, or exits the soccer world cup, or loses at rugby, etc. Odd, really, since inventing a sport ought not to have any implications for a country's ability to play it well.

Be that as it may, the purpose here is merely to note the roles played by England in the invention or development of the best known and best loved sports in the world.

Football (Soccer)

No one would be so bold as to claim that England was necessarily the first place where a pig's bladder was inflated and kicked about the place. Indeed, it is clear that the practice of kicking or otherwise propelling some sort of ball towards an opponent's goal or line easily pre-dates Anglo-Saxon England, since it is known to have been a pastime in ancient China, ancient Greece and Rome. And yet England can certainly claim to have formulated the rules of the game of Association Football, and given them to the world.

An attempt to standardize the rules of the game in England was made at Cambridge University in 1843, and in 1846 most public schools (where the game was very popular) adopted "The Cambridge Rules". In 1862 and 1863 the rules were published by a number of football clubs in the London area, and the Football Association was founded.

Association football was "exported" by English sailors, merchants and businessmen in the course of their travels abroad, spreading widely in Europe and to the now fanatical shores of South America before the end of the nineteenth century.

In 1888, the Football League was formed by 12 clubs who were using professional players at that time, and in due course other leagues along the English model were formed in France, Germany, Holland, Argentina and Brazil.

In a typical example of English snobbery, the Football Association declined to become a founder member of FIFA (*Federation Internationale de Football Associations*) in 1904, but joined two years later.

Cricket

As in the case of football, no one would suggest that England was necessarily the first place where a stone or some sort of hard sphere of matted material was batted about the place with a stick, and yet England can again claim to have formulated the rules of the game of cricket, and given them to the world (or, at least, to the Commonwealth).

The earliest reference to an eleven-a-side game of cricket is dated 1697 (played in Sussex); the first match between two counties was played in 1709 (Kent vs Surrey - and no doubt some cricket maniac could tell you the score if you asked!), and the first important set of rules is dated 1744. The Marylebone Cricket Club was founded in 1787, and remains the spiritual headquarters of world cricket. The first English team to tour abroad did so in 1859.

The game was exported empire-wide in the manner of football. The founder members of the Imperial Cricket Conference (1909) were England, Australia and South Africa, and these countries were joined in due course by India, New Zealand, the West Indies and Pakistan. The successor body to the Conference, now named the International Cricket Council (based in London), has since taken in many other countries, including some non-Commonwealth countries.

Rugby - Union and League

England (specifically, Rugby School) can obviously claim to have invented rugby football.

William Webb Ellis is alleged to be the famous cheat who "invented" the game of rugby in 1823, by picking up the ball during a game of soccer at Rugby school and running with it. Be that as it may, rules of the new game were published at that school in 1846, and the game caught on throughout England, and also in Wales, Scotland and Ireland. The (English) Rugby Football Union was formed in 1871.

The game spread abroad in the usual manner, through the efforts of British sailors, merchants, businessmen and so on. Rugby has proved itself to have wider appeal than cricket amongst non-Commonwealth countries, being played with fervour in such countries as France, Italy, Romania, Argentina and Japan.

In 1895, twenty-two clubs from the north of England seceded from the Rugby Football Union over the issue of professionalism, and formed what became known as the Rugby Football League. In due course, the rules of rugby league parted company with those of rugby union, as attempts were made to open up the game and make it more attractive to spectators, in response to the financial pressures always implicit in the professional game.

This version of the game has had less world-wide appeal than Union, but is popular in England, France, New Zealand, Australia and Papua New Guinea.

Squash

A descendant of rackets, and generally believed to have developed at Harrow School, in England, in the mid-nineteenth century. By the early twentieth century the sport had spread widely to other schools and to the public, and squash clubs had been formed at Bath, and at the Marylebone Cricket Club.

The sport was spread widely throughout the British empire by expatriates, and has since spread to many other countries.

Tennis

There seems to be some debate over who "invented" modern tennis; it may have been an Englishman in 1872, or a Welshman in 1873. Be that as it may, the Marylebone Cricket Club published a set of rules for the game in 1875.

Around that time, the All-England Croquet Club, based at Wimbledon, set aside one of its croquet lawns for tennis, and changed its name to the All-England Croquet and Lawn Tennis Club. In 1877 the club held a championship, having devised court dimensions and rules which are still extant.

National championships were first held in America in 1881; in France in 1891; and in Australia in 1905.

Hockey

Rudimentary versions of the game of hockey are known to have been played by the Persians, Greeks, Romans and Arabs, amongst others.

In England the first hockey club existed at least as early as 1861, and the rules of the modern game were codified in London in 1886 by the newly formed Hockey Association. The rule concerning sticks not coming above shoulder height dates from this period, as does the change from a rubber cube to a ball, and the introduction of the shooting circle.

The British Army spread the game widely, particularly in the Indian sub-continent and in the Far East, and international competition commenced in 1895.

Badminton

Badminton takes its name from the seat of the Dukes of Beaufort in England, where the game of badminton is said to have been developed in 1873.

The game was exported primarily by British Army officers, most notably to India and South-East Asia.

The first All-England championships were held in 1899, and the International Badminton Federation was formed in 1934, in England.

Boxing

Pugilism has presumably existed for as long as mankind, and is certainly noted by many ancient sources. Thus, England should not claim any special place in the genesis of the sport of boxing *per se*.

However, the modern sport's first set of rules was developed in England in 1743, and a further major development came with the London Prize Ring rules of 1838, accepted in both Britain and America. By this time rudimentary gloves were worn, and kicking, butting, gouging, biting, low blows and hitting a man while down were illegal.

A new set of rules was developed in 1867 by the Amateur Athletic Club, and these have become known as the Queensberry rules because of the patronage provided them by the 9th Marquess of Queensberry. The new rules differed in four principal ways from the London Prize Ring rules: padded gloves were worn; rounds were limited to three minutes plus a minute's rest; wrestling was illegal; and a 10 second knock-out rule was introduced. Weight divisions were also introduced.

Footnote on American Football and Baseball

American Football derives from soccer (which arrived with English colonists in the seventeenth century), and from rugby. It is a matter of seemingly endless debate where the first game of American football was actually played in the United States, but it is known that a "football" game played between Harvard and Yale universities in 1876 was played in the carrying rather than kicking style. That same year, representatives from Harvard, Yale, Columbia and Princeton universities met to agree a set of rules for the new game, and it is from this source that the modern game of American Football has developed.

Baseball seems to be a derivative of the English game of rounders, which is very similar in nature to baseball. A set of rules for the American game, which clearly drew upon the rules of rounders (known in the United States from at least 1834), was developed in New York in 1845, and after the American Civil War these rules were accepted as the definitive rules across the nation.

Conclusion

It is perhaps only cricket, rugby, squash and badminton which can be reliably thought of as English "inventions", but in all of the sports mentioned above England has clearly played a pivotal role.

This cannot be attributed to any native sporting talent on the part of the English, but must be attributed to the broad political and economic prestige which England enjoyed in the eighteenth and nineteenth centuries, when these sports were being developed and codified.

Here again we find England's story woven into the stuff of other people's lives: big sporting events like the soccer, rugby and cricket world cups, or the Superbowl or baseball finals in the United States are watched by hundreds of millions of people all around the world. Similarly, countless millions of people attend local sports matches every week, or play these sports in their back yards. And in every case, once again, a direct link to England can be found.

Chapter 6

OTHER ENGLISH CONTRIBUTIONS

Introduction

The crucial topics of constitutional history, law and the English language have so far been covered, along with the more trivial subject (some would say) of sport. This chapter rounds off this section of the book with a look at a number of further ways in which England's story finds itself woven into the stuff of so many people's lives.

The Greenwich Meridian

It has long been possible to determine a ship's latitude north or south of the equator by use of an angle measuring device (such as a sextant) and knowledge of the sun's declination (its "height" or position relative to the equator, on any particular day).

When, in the eighteenth century, time pieces were developed which could travel aboard ships without being affected by their motion, it also became relatively straightforward to determine a ship's longitude with accuracy. This is done by comparing a ship's local time against a fixed datum, which in the case of the British Navy was the time at the Greenwich Meridian (a line which runs from the North Pole through the original site of the Greenwich Observatory in London, to the South Pole). The Greenwich Observatory was founded in 1675 by Charles II to provide the English Navy with the information necessary for these longitudinal calculations.

With the increase in international travel in the nineteenth century, and in particular the advent of railways, it became clear to the international community that time would need to be standardised, so that time-tabling complications across borders could be resolved. Therefore, in 1883 the concept of Standard Time was developed by international agreement, and Greenwich Time was selected as the world's datum. The world was divided into 24 time zones, and all time zones are now described as being so many hours east or west of Greenwich. At about the same time the Greenwich Meridian was adopted as the datum for longitude, meaning that all other longitudes would be defined as east or west of Greenwich, by all countries.

Thus, Greenwich provides the world's location datum, and time datum. The choice of the Greenwich Meridian and Greenwich Mean Time as the data against which longitude and time would henceforth be measured was not forced upon the world by Britain, of course. However, the economic, military and diplomatic status of Britain at that time, and the long history of astronomical data available from the Greenwich Observatory, made Greenwich the natural choice.

Science and the Arts

England has of course produced some noteworthy scientists - Roger Bacon, Newton, Darwin, Lister and Faraday spring to mind. However, many countries have produced noteworthy scientists, and England should not claim any special preeminence in this field. Similarly, England's contribution to the arts has been substantial - Shakespeare, Dickens, Tennyson, Shelley, Keats, Wordsworth, Turner, Gainsborough, Constable - but England has no especial monopoly on artistic talent either, and no implication of unique genius could be inferred even if she did.

Making general inferences about a country's significance based on the scientific or artistic achievements of its citizens confuses causes with effects, in the author's opinion - countries do not operate on level playing fields in these matters. To a considerable degree the ability of a nation to fund cerebral and aesthetic activity, and the viability of cerebral and aesthetic careers, generally depend upon a country having a certain economic critical mass.

To that extent, England's achievements in the fields of science and the arts ("the effects") yet again derive from her broader history ("the cause").

Freedom, Liberty and the Rule of Law

General

England has enjoyed a pragmatic and theoretically fair system of laws for a good deal longer than other countries, and generally circumscribed the absolute powers of her rulers somewhat earlier than was done elsewhere. She thus began establishing in her people's minds a respect for legal process well before most other nations. This is perhaps why the concept of the rule of law is so deeply fixed in the psyche of the English and British people, and is probably the ultimate reason for the long (though far from perfect) tradition of freedom and liberty of the subject which characterizes the English system as a whole. Consider Trevelyan, discussing the extensive judicial reforms and innovations of Henry II (discussed in chapter 3): "It was owing to Henry of Anjou (Henry II) that anarchy was quelled in the early morning of our history, instead of the late noon, as happened in the feudal lands of the continent".

The right to trial by jury; the idea that a jury should be made up of one's peers; the concept of *Habeus Corpus* - all of these things are fundamental to the English (and now British) way of life, and yet are foreign to many jurisdictions around the world. This is a matter of which Englishmen should be very proud.

The right to personal freedom flows directly from Magna Carta, the Petition of Right and the Bill of Rights, all cited in chapter 3. In particular, the Bill of Rights ended forever the periodic attempts by the Crown to rule through controlled courts handing down arbitrary decisions.

The English press has been free from general censorship and control since 1692, when Parliament refused to renew the Licencing Act, which had started life under Elizabeth I (in 1586) as a restriction on any book being published before it had been read and approved by the authorities.

The basic fairness of the institutions which England had developed for herself by the end of the seventeenth century can be attested to by the willingness of the Dutch and other foreigners to live under English authority in the American colonies. This bode well (though the English were not yet thinking in these terms) for the establishment of a British empire composed of many races and religions. It might be noted that the colonies of other European nations were developing along much more authoritarian and centralized lines at the same time, offering neither religious nor political freedom from their "home" governments.

Thus by the end of the seventeenth century the English system can be clearly differentiated from those of the continent through the existence of parliamentary democracy, and of freedoms of the individual and of the press.

It was at about this same time that England was victorious over

Louis XIV's France, and this fact was widely noted, and did much to create the intellectual movement against despotism which flourished in the eighteenth century.

Some specific examples of English freedoms and philanthropy follow:

Habeus Corpus Act 1679

Habeus Corpus looks back directly to Clause 39 of Magna Carta (reproduced above), and in 1679 the concept of *Habeus Corpus* was formally introduced into the English legal system. *Habeus Corpus* is a motion demanding that an imprisoned person be brought before the courts, so that the validity of their incarceration can be tested.

Habeus Corpus has entered into many constitutions or legal systems around the world. For example, Article 1, Section 9, Clause 2 of the United States' constitution provides that "the writ of *Habeus Corpus* shall not be suspended, unless when in cases of rebellion or invasion the public safety may require it".

In England in 1816, *Habeus Corpus* was extended to cover persons confined other than on a criminal charge, and the concept now lies right at the heart of public liberty in many countries of the world. It thus ensures (or ought to ensure) that despots and dictators in many places around the world do not incarcerate political enemies or other "undesirables" indefinitely.

Whilst on the subject of the rights of the accused in England, it should be mentioned that the accused has been entitled to counsel since 1836, and has had the right to testify on his own behalf since 1898. The right of appeal against criminal convictions was created in 1907.

Free Trade

England led the world in the fight for trade liberalization, which it commenced doing in the first half of the nineteenth century. The fight was focused on the Corn Laws, which was a system of tariffs designed to protect the English farmer from cheap imports (as can be seen in the European Union today, tariff barriers have wide appeal amongst inefficient producers, and so the fight continues). The idea of free trade had to struggle against the enterprise-stunting belief, which had been widely held throughout the world for centuries, that there was only a certain amount of trade to be had. Those who held this opinion - they were called mercantilists - consequently thought it a proper function of government to protect a country's existing producers, lest that country's entire productive capacity fall victim to competitive foreigners. After much vigorous resistance from vested farming interests, the Corn Laws were repealed in England in 1846, at a time when protectionists still remained very much in the ascendancy elsewhere.

Abolition of Slavery

The trafficking of black slaves by Europeans was not the only slave trade, but only the best known. Neither was England the first country or the last to employ slavery. However, fortunately for our collective conscience, we did play a leading role in its abolition, in both a direct sense (throughout the British empire) and in a moral sense elsewhere (through example or persuasion).

The first black slaves were brought to Europe by the Portuguese in 1444, and until the mid-sixteenth century black slaves were employed in Europe itself, or in the Spanish and Portuguese Atlantic islands. From the mid-sixteenth century onwards Europeans began to transport black slaves to the New World in large numbers, and England was only one of several players in this high growth and profitable business.

The Enlightenment of the eighteenth century slowly led to a general discomfort about slavery amongst those who thought about such things, and societies were formed in various places to agitate for the ending of the trade. Britain acquired Sierra Leone in 1787, and it was soon used by English philanthropists as a home for freed slaves. Britain abolished its slave trade in 1807, and slavery itself in all British dominions in 1833 (cf. France 1848, the United States 1865). This achievement stands very much to the credit of everyone involved, particularly since under the war conditions of 1807, political agitation was not permitted. It would seem that somehow the conscience and collective will of the British people could still be brought to bear, even in such critical times.

Moreover, at the end of the Napoleonic wars (1815) Britain was in a unique diplomatic and maritime position to persuade the European powers that the slave trade should be suppressed generally, and it was fortuitous indeed that this was agreed to before the interior of Africa was developed by those powers later in the nineteenth century.

Much credit for this magnificent contribution to civilization must go to England's William Wilberforce, and to the achievements of Britain's soldiers, sailors and statesmen, who put their country in a position to be able to do something about it.

Abolition of Suttee and Female Infanticide in India

Suttee is an ancient Hindu custom which expects a widow to burn herself to death on her husband's funeral pyre. It has been practiced widely all over India from at least the year 510 AD, and survived some ineffectual Moghul attempts to prohibit it. Suttee was finally abolished throughout British India in 1829, and it may be assumed that this came as a considerable relief to a large number of long-living Indian females.

It should also be mentioned in passing that the British Raj proscribed the ever-popular form of Indian social engineering known as female infanticide, although it could never be, and has never been, stamped out completely.

The Howard League for Penal Reform

John Howard (1726-1790) was appointed high sheriff of Bedfordshire in 1773, and soon became appalled by the condition of the county's prisons and prisoners. He caused certain statutes to be passed through the House of Commons improving the rights and sanitary condition of prisoners throughout Britain. He died in the Ukraine, whilst conducting a fatal investigation into the causes and possible cures for the plague and similar ailments.

The Howard League for Penal Reform is an amalgamation of the Howard Association, set up in England independently of John Howard in 1866 and named in his honour, and the Penal Reform League, set up in England in 1907. It is an independent charity relying entirely on voluntary contributions, and works for humane and rational reform of criminal justice and penal systems. The English Howard League has counterparts in New Zealand, Canada and (strange as it may seem) Panama.

Trade Unionism, etc.

The world's earliest fraternal self-help organizations for working men were set up in England in the eighteenth century. British trade unionists exhibited a unique and early preference for political (as opposed to revolutionary) action, and this tendency led naturally to the Trades Union Congress and the Independent Labour Party forming the Labour Representation Committee in 1900 (renamed the Labour Party in 1906). British trade unionists were obliged to travel a very hard and unsympathetic road for a very long time, but their tradition of constitutionality must be taken as a back-handed compliment to a system which was just sufficiently responsive just sufficiently often for those persons who favoured a more revolutionary approach to never gain wide support in Britain.

Britain was also the first country to regulate the conditions under which her workers toiled in her factories, and was the cradle of the cooperative movement, which did such sterling service in training the working classes in thrift, mutual assistance, and business practices.

Toleration of Karl Marx (1818-1883)

Whatever the reader's view about Karl Marx and Marxism may be, it can be readily appreciated that his works and philosophies must have been deeply offensive to the entire political hierarchy of nineteenth century England. It can therefore be taken as an indication of the fundamental liberality of the English system that he was allowed to settle and publish in England (having been kicked out of a number of European countries). Marx spent more than half of his sixty five years in England, published his most important work (*Das Kapital*) whilst resident, and is buried in London.

Driving on the left

A trivial thing, it might seem, but two and a half billion people do it, mostly because of the English[3].

It seems clear from some recent research conducted at the site of a Roman quarry in England (where light carts would have entered, and heavy ones would have left) that the Romans drove on the left. That driving on the left should be "normal" is intuitively believable in any case, because the majority of the world's population appears to have always been right-handed (as far as can be told from statuary and art), and passing an oncoming rider or pedestrian right-to-right would be logical if one foresaw the possibility of having to draw one's sword or other weapon in defence.

Thus the "keep left" rule cannot be claimed as an invention by England (let's face it, there were only ever two options to choose from)! Having said that, as the most populous home nation and the seat of government, it is England which will have decided the issue on a formal basis within the United Kingdom (if there was ever any disagreement on the matter), and it was Britain which exported a formal keep left rule to the Commonwealth countries (including Canada, until it decided it couldn't swim against the American tide any longer). Incidentally, it appears that it was Napoleon who decided that "keep right" should be the rule within his empire (and thus in certain formerly French colonies, and in South America, via Spain and Portugal). The United States seems to have adopted "keep right" either in a spirit of fraternal revolutionary solidarity with the French, or just to be plain contrary.

Here again we have a manifestation of England's history affecting hundreds of millions of people every day (actually, about two and a half billion people), from Scotland to

New Zealand, and from South-East Asia through India to most of sub-Saharan Africa, without them even thinking about it. Even in those countries where there was sufficient vehicular traffic to have required traffic rules before the coming of the English/British, it will have been British laws which made the "keep left" rule an established fact within those countries, the effect of which can be seen on their roads every day.

The Industrial Revolution

Banking supremacy lay in the hands of English bankers by the end of the seventeenth century. At about that same time, life insurance was developing (with all that is implicit in the consequent accumulation of large, liquid reserves), and the forerunners of the London Stock Exchange were quoting the securities of joint stock companies. Thus in London there developed a preeminent centre of financial excellence and innovation, ready to finance the industrial expansion of the next century.

It can be justly claimed that "industrialization" is an English invention, since it was in England that the characteristic combination of new materials with new energy sources, new inventions, the factory system and a widespread transport system first appeared. In the period 1760 to 1830 the Industrial Revolution was essentially confined to Britain. Indeed, the British went out of their way to minimize cross-fertilization of other European economies, but in due course this inevitably happened. In Europe, industrialization first took place in Belgium just after the turn of the nineteenth century, through the efforts of two English entrepreneurs, and later spread to France. The rest of Europe lagged considerably behind these three countries, through impoverishment and because of political situations which were not conducive to economic activity and investment. However, by the turn of the twentieth century Germany was becoming a force to be reckoned with, as was America.

The Church of England

The Church of England as a Protestant institution originates with Henry VIII's break with Rome in 1534, despite the fact that it remained a Catholic Church in his day. Protestant reforms were introduced during the reign of Henry's son Edward VI, and following a pause given to its development by Mary I's persecutions, Elizabeth I introduced the Book of Common Prayer and the Thirty-Nine Articles, defining the liturgy and doctrine of the Protestant Church.

There are nearly seventy million members of the Anglican Church, in a total of one hundred and sixty four countries. During the first stage of its foreign dissemination, Anglicanism was established by English and British colonization in countries such as the USA, Canada, Southern Africa, Australia and New Zealand. The second stage of development started at the end of the nineteenth century, involving the establishment of Anglican Churches in other countries, as a result of missionary work by the "home country" Churches, and the colonies' Churches.

The Anglican Churches around the world have been involved in a process of decentralisation of authority for over two hundred years, but "remain linked by mutual affection and loyalty", we are told. The Archbishop of Canterbury, resident in London, is the focus of Anglican unity, and convenes a conference at his palace in Lambeth every decade, this being the principal means by which unity of policy is maintained.

The Salvation Army

The Salvation Army is a Protestant, evangelical, charitable organization operated along military lines, with its international headquarters in London. It was set up by William Booth in 1865 in the East End of London (although it did not operate under its current name until 1878), and now operates more than three thousand soup kitchens, hospitals, schools, and other welfare institutions in over eighty countries.

Boy Scouts and Girl Guides

Another couple of things which might seem trivial to some people, but to many people who have been Boy Scouts or Girl Guides, they can be very serious issues! The Boy Scouts organization was set up in 1908 by Lord Baden-Powell, and the Girl Guides in 1910, by he and his wife and sister. There are now Scouting and Guiding organizations in more than one hundred and ten countries, and there are countless millions of people all around the world who have sworn an oath of fidelity, at one time or another, to these quaint creations of an old English soldier.

Foreign place names

English towns and famous Englishmen are commemorated throughout the English speaking world through places named after them, and a selection of the better known places (if not, necessarily, the better known Englishmen) are listed below. It should be noted that there are also many places around the world named after members of the Royal family (Victoria, Alberta, Georgia, Adelaide, Maryland, Charleston, Charlotte, Jamestown, etc.), but these have been omitted on the grounds that there are few people less English (or, at least, less Anglo-Saxon) in England than the British Royal family!

United States of America:

The Hudson River (Henry Hudson, navigator), Pittsburgh (William Pitt the Elder, statesman), New York (since 1664), New England, New Hampshire, New Jersey (but note that Jersey is not, strictly speaking, part of England), Washington (named after George Washington, of course, but his surname is itself English in origin, the ending *-ington* being one of the classic Anglo-Saxon place name endings, along with *-ing*, *-ings*, and *-ingham*), Pennsylvania (William Penn, Quaker), Boston (Boston, Lincolnshire), Norfolk (Norfolk County), Richmond (Richmond upon Thames), Raleigh (Sir Walter Raleigh, adventurer), London, Cambridge, Birmingham, etc., etc.;

Canada:

Hudson Bay (Henry Hudson again), London (Ontario), Vancouver (Captain George Vancouver RN, navigator), Halifax (George Montagu Dunk, 2nd Earl of Halifax, President of the Board of Trade in 1749), etc., etc;

Australia:

Sydney (Lord Thomas Townshend Sydney, British Home Secretary in 1788), Melbourne (Lord Melbourne, British Prime Minister in 1837), Darwin (Charles Darwin, scientist), Phillip Island (Captain Arthur Phillip RN, first Governor of New South Wales), Furneaux Group (Tobias Furneaux RN, navigator), Bass Strait (George Bass RN, surgeon-explorer), Norfolk Island (Duke of Norfolk), etc., etc.;

New Zealand:

Auckland (George Eden, 2nd Earl of Auckland, First Lord of the Admiralty), Christchurch (Christ Church College, Oxford, alma mater of a leading light in the Canterbury Association which settled Christchurch), Cook's Strait (Captain James Cook RN, navigator), Nelson (Admiral Lord Nelson RN, naval hero), Hastings (Warren Hastings, first Governor-General of British India), Palmerston North (Lord Palmerston, British Prime Minister), Banks Peninsula (Sir Joseph Banks, botanist on Captain Cook's first voyage), etc., etc.

Commentary

And so we find a host of further ways in which England's story is woven into the stuff of other people's lives. Amongst other things, all mariners and pilots fix their positions and time zones with reference to a place in England; any inhabitant of a Commonwealth country or the United States of America who finds himself in trouble with the law can thank England for the concept of *Habeus Corpus*; almost everyone who drives on the left hand side of the road is doing so because of England; all Boy Scouts and Girl Guides can blame an Englishman for having to camp out in the rain; convicts, trade unionists, Anglicans, and down-and-outs find succour in organizations born in England; and many people living in the United States, Canada, Australia and New Zealand (in particular) can even thank some English person or English place for the name of their home town!

Part Three

Myths and Reality

INTRODUCTION

The greatest crime that any historian can commit is to invent history; the second greatest crime is to fail to see historical events in proper context.

It is clear that England has come into more extensive contact with more foreign nations, to more lasting effect, than any other country on earth. As a natural result, her history as it has affected these other nations, from those as near as Scotland to those as far away as New Zealand, has perhaps been subjected to closer and more exhaustive scrutiny than that of any other country.

The English have been accused of many crimes, follies and injustices over the years, and this litany of alleged abuses seems to have succeeded in undermining the self-confidence of the English people, and of the descendants of English colonists in the English-speaking countries. It seems no longer politically correct to be proud to be English or of English ancestry; one must instead be ashamed of all the terrible things which were allegedly done to England's/Britain's "victims" all over the world. Conversely, it seems positively fashionable these days for one's ancestors to have been "victims" of English or British aggression (now that these matters can be viewed from a comfortably safe distance).

Whilst much of what is said about England's relationships with these other countries may well be true, there are also many myths, legends and half-truths floating around which don't actually stand up to close scrutiny. It should always be kept in mind that many of these myths, legends and half-truths are perpetuated by people with political agendas (such as some Scots, Welsh, and Irish separatists within the United Kingdom, and various indigenous peoples elsewhere), whose own purposes may be well served by denigrating the English and engendering feelings of pride and nationhood amongst their fellow countrymen.

The following two chapters deal in some detail with the histories of Ireland and Scotland vis-à-vis England, and then more briefly with those of various indigenous races which have come into contact with the English at one time or another. The purpose here is to examine critically the nature of the relationships between the English and these nations, with a view to encouraging some clear and more realistic thinking about these matters, and debunking some of the more tiresome myths which persist about them.

Chapter 7

IRELAND AND SCOTLAND

Ireland

The author has been told by certain Irish friends and relations that the citizens of the Republic of Ireland fall into three camps, as far as their attitudes to the English are concerned. Members of the first group have much the same attitude to England as many English people presently have to Germany: we're all friends now, we're all part of Europe, let's forget any historical difficulties and just get on with getting on. This group needs no further attention here, except that a moment should be taken to applaud their enlightened and sensible attitude.

A second group of Irish people apparently harbour a specific and continuing resentment over the partition of Ireland into six predominantly Protestant counties and twenty-six predominantly Catholic counties in 1922. This group should reflect upon the facts that there were and are serious tensions between some Protestants and some Catholics in Ireland, and that for at least ten years before the signing of the Anglo-Irish Treaty in 1921 there had been every reason to believe that if some sort of demarcation between the Protestant Irish and the Catholic Irish was not effected, a Balkan-style war was a distinct possibility. It should be remembered that there have been Protestants in all parts of Ireland longer than there have been Irish people in any part of the United States - and presumably few Irish people (and few Irish-Americans) advocate all the Irish being kicked out of America. If that is so, then these same people must accept that after some unspecified number of centuries have passed, pragmatism or plain common sense dictates that physical presence in a country grants ancient immigrants some right of domicile. If that fact *is* accepted, but nevertheless war between two mutually antagonistic populations seems inevitable if they are not kept apart, then partition is surely a fair and reasonable solution. By 1921 Ulster had already effectively evolved into a separate State and already had a functioning parliament by virtue of the Government of Ireland Act 1920. The Anglo-Irish Treaty simply recognized the *de facto* division of Ireland into two parts: the north-east which was broadly Protestant, and the rest of Ireland which was broadly Catholic. When all is said and done, the Anglo-Irish Treaty which was approved by the Dail Eireann in January 1922 was a *negotiated compromise* between the British government and the Dail and, despite its failings, it seemed the best solution available at the time to an otherwise insoluble problem.

This brings us to the ancient history which caused Protestants to come to Ireland in the first place, and it brings us to the third group of Irish people, who apparently harbour a more general resentment of the English, based on a vague and often limited understanding of this history. Some political mischief-makers in Ireland and around the world do their best to encourage and maintain a hatred of the English based upon that race's real and imagined behaviour towards the Irish. Before examining Ireland's most immortal myths (those surrounding the famine), let us first recall that "England's" involvement in Ireland commenced in 1169 at the request of Dermot, King of Leinster, who invited some Cambro-Norman mercenaries over to Ireland to assist him in his fight with two other Irish kings. The Cambro-Normans were not the sort of people to let a monumental blunder like that pass them by, so they accepted Dermot's kind invitation and, acting largely on their own account, they colonized Leinster and County Meath, and settled there. King Henry II, concerned at the possibility of an independent Norman kingdom in Ireland, landed near Waterford in 1171, and received oaths of loyalty from the Cambro-Normans, and from a number of Irish kings and chiefs, who preferred distant rule by an English king to more "in-yer-face" rule by a neighbouring Irish king. The Cambro-Norman noblemen and their Anglo-Norman cousins occupied the fertile valleys of east and south-east Ireland, and brought much of the rest of Ireland under their effective political control. They were followed in the fourteenth and fifteenth centuries by a second wave of settlers - English lawyers, merchants, administrators, priests, farmers, craftsmen, and so on - and all of these colonists together (i.e. the Normans and the English) are sometimes referred to as the "Old English", to distinguish them from later *Protestant* settlers.

The Old English were firm adherents to English legal procedures, they spoke English, and they were loyal to the English Crown, but they can be ignored here for a number of reasons. Firstly, because they were (and mostly remained) Catholic. Secondly, because they intermarried and effectively became Irish in every respect (although it would have long horrified them to have been so described). And thirdly, because their leaders became classic "over-mighty" subjects who came to resent interference by the English kings in what they considered to be their own private domain, and were thus early leaders of conservative "Irish" resistance to English rule. Later, they were also leaders (along with the Old English clergy) of the Catholic Irish resistance to the Reformation. Really, it obscures rather than clarifies to think of the Old English as English - it quickly became no more accurate to say that they were English than it would be to say that a Mexican is a Spaniard.

It is the third wave of colonists who were and are the problem: Protestants from England and Scotland. It must be remembered that after the English and Scottish Reformations, politics and religion became inextricably intertwined, and the stakes (a good choice of word) could not have been higher. In particular, Catholicism became connected in the English mind not only with Irish resistance to English rule, but also with the Spanish Inquisition, Bloody Mary, Philip of Spain, and basically the very survival of the Protestant English monarchy and the system of government which the English were developing for themselves by the seventeenth century. Unfortunately, fear, greed and religious bigotry are dangerous bed-fellows, and many atrocities would henceforward be committed by both sides in Ireland - or it might be better to say all *three* sides: the Catholic Irish, the Protestant Irish, and the English forces.

As a response to various anti-Reformation and anti-English rebellions, Protestants were encouraged to settle in Ireland and colonize the place from the sixteenth century onwards, and the Catholic Irish (including, it is worthy of note, the Old English) were systematically disenfranchised and dispossessed. As early as in the reign of Elizabeth I, English monarchs were not unnaturally insisting that all people in their service should acknowledge their spiritual as well as temporal authority, and this had the effect of disbarring Catholics from royal administrative office, which meant that English Protestants slowly replaced Catholics as jobs became vacant in the Dublin administration. Gaelic lords who would not acknowledge the English Crown as sovereign and generally facilitate the Anglicization of their domains were also dispossessed and replaced by English officers.

Private schemes of colonization, sometimes backed by private armies, were encouraged by the Protestant administrators in Dublin. Occasionally, when the Crown or Parliament had to intervene militarily in Ireland, English colonists were settled on the confiscated lands of rebel noblemen. One extreme example of royal confiscation following rebellion came under James I, where (after a few years' delay for various reasons) the defeat of

Hugh O'Neill's Irish-Spanish army in 1601 was followed by widespread English and Scottish settlement upon forfeited lands. Settlement took place in all four Irish provinces, but was particularly heavy in Ulster, where an uncompromising Scottish Presbyterianism came to predominate. Catholic landowners all over Ireland - including the Old English - came to be seen as, by definition, rebellious or potentially rebellious, and were zealously expropriated by the Protestant officials in Dublin, and replaced by Protestant settlers from Britain. Following the rebellion of 1641, Oliver Cromwell invaded Ireland and when he had summarily crushed all military resistance, a second extreme example of Catholic dispossession was executed: all Catholic estates east of the Shannon were confiscated, and settled upon Cromwell's soldiers and upon those persons who had financed his operations in Ireland. After the defeat of James II's forces in 1690-91, confiscation of Catholic lands west of the Shannon largely completed the nationwide extirpation of the Catholic landed interest. Thus by the turn of the eighteenth century, the social elite in Ireland was exclusively Protestant in religion, and was composed of first generation settlers from England or Scotland, descendants of earlier Protestant settlers, and descendants of a few Old English and Gaelic families who had converted to the Protestant faith.

In considering all of these matters, it should be remembered that Ireland was a foreign country (or a rebellious colony, depending on one's point of view), and there was nothing in the rule books in those days which required any country to view a neighbouring country with feelings of charity, compassion and respect for their property and persons. Was it not Irish pirates who carried off the young man who became Saint Patrick from his home near Bristol and made him a slave in Ireland, and did not the ancient Irish tribe called the Scots successfully invade the country which now bears their name? Let us keep a bit of perspective here; Ireland was a constant source of rebellion and trouble to England, and served as a springboard for a number of invasions, and as a sanctuary for various of her enemies, from time to time. Therefore it can be legitimately asked why the English in historical times should have had any reason at all to feel charitably disposed towards the Irish. In 1534, the Old English earls of Kildare rose in rebellion at the very moment when Henry VIII was breaking with Rome; Hugh O'Neill rebelled in 1601; in 1641, the Catholics rebelled at a time when England was already embroiled in the constitutional crisis which would very shortly lead to civil war; they gave succour to James II and a French army after the Glorious Revolution; they rebelled again in 1798 during the Napoleonic Wars; and again in 1916, during the First World War. One might say that only a fool would have chosen any other times to rebel against so mighty a foe as England but, nevertheless, one can hardly expect these rebellions to have done anything to endear the Irish to their more powerful neighbours. Ireland also exported (and still exports) large numbers of her workers to England, with the result that the pitiful wages of the eighteenth and nineteenth century industrial worker, labourer and farm-hand in England came under repeated downwards pressure. This not unnaturally engendered a widespread antipathy towards the Irish, and even led to numerous anti-Irish riots during those centuries. All in all, not a history which can be thought of as particularly endearing, from an English point of view.

It would not be possible to justify the invasion and colonization of Ireland by English and Scottish Protestants under today's international laws any more than it would be possible to justify the seizure of Pictish territory in Scotland by the Irish Scots, or any Irish king's attack upon any other's territory. The rules of international diplomacy were somewhat more accommodating of the ambitious colonist in those days, and Ireland would no doubt have returned the favour if the boot had been on the other foot. As suggested above, the importation of foreign Protestants into Ireland is now a centuries-old established fact, and nothing can be achieved by railing against that circumstance now. By all rational uses of the word, these foreigners also became Irish in due course and their descendants, along with those of the Old English, now make up a goodly proportion of the total population of Ireland.

This brings us to closer examination of that schizophrenic breed, the Anglo-Irish - although it would be better to call them the Protestant-Irish, since we are talking about Protestants from both Scotland and England, and we are *not* talking about the Old English, most of whom remained Catholic. In due course the Protestant colonists intermarried, of course, and became to any outsider's eyes fully Irish. It was they who were "on the ground", doing most of the dispossessing and discriminating which is so rightly complained of. There was a general view amongst the Anglo-Irish "Ascendancy" that the London government was "soft" on the Catholic question, and the Ascendancy often had to push for anti-Catholic legislation in the face of British reluctance. A certain section of the Ascendancy would always remain vehement in its resistance to the ideas of Catholic emancipation and Irish Home Rule - and yet it was also members of the Ascendancy who campaigned *for* Catholic emancipation and led the push *for* Irish autonomy and Home Rule (at least until Catholic nationalists were in a position to predominate). So were the members of the generally paranoid and bigoted Anglo-Irish Ascendancy British or were they Irish? Ethnically, they certainly became both, but politically the question is more difficult. Both the Celtic Irish and the British thought the Anglo-Irish were too much in the other's camp for their liking, but if the modern Irish are going to claim as their own (as they constantly do) such great Anglo-Irish personalities as Jonathan Swift, George Bernard Shaw, Oscar Wilde, William Butler Yeats, Edmund Burke, Richard Brinsley Sheridan, the Duke of Wellington, and even Henry Grattan, Wolfe Tone and

Charles Stewart Parnell - then they can claim the whole sorry lot of the gerrymandering, discriminating and bigoted Anglo-Irish, which would put a rather different slant on things.

The reader may infer from the tone of the above comments that the author does not have a great deal of sympathy for the Anglo-Irish, and it would certainly appear to be the case that they have a lot to answer for. However, there is a danger here of being "holier than thou" from a safe distance. The last major plantation of Protestants took place more than three hundred years ago, and these people intermingled and intermarried, and eventually became to all intents and purposes Irish, with no other home to go to. And yet they had to get by knowing that the very fact of their presence in Ireland remained in dispute, and they lived cheek by jowl with Catholics for centuries in an environment of mutual fear and distrust, sometimes on the receiving end of, and sometimes perpetrating, atrocities. As has already been stated, the fact that English and Scottish people settled on land expropriated from prior owners (note the use of the word "prior" rather than "native", since many of those dispossessed were Old English) should long since have ceased to be a cause of outrage. All nations played fast and loose with other nations' rights in those days, including the Gaelic Irish who practiced dispossession and murder upon the Picts in Scotland, and upon each other in Ireland, until the Old English put a stop to them doing it, and started doing it themselves. Is it not hypocritical and pointless to claim that it is an especial outrage that England and Scotland played by these same rules, or are theft and murder OK just as long as you are not on the receiving end?

With all of these thoughts in mind, let us now turn to the events of the 1840s. If the reader will pardon the pun, there is a load of rot talked about the potato famine. The bald facts are well known: that the failure of the potato crops in 1845-46 was followed by famine, disease and death on an appalling scale, and that these proceedings caused widespread resentment against landlords. The points which need to be made here are as follows:

Firstly, there were far more Irish landlords (that is, Anglo-Irish and a few Gaelic Irish) than English landlords, and they were just as insensitive as the English ones. The issue was fundamentally a class issue, not a racial one - the nineteenth century English peasant was treated with exactly the same contempt and disregard for human dignity as the Irish peasant (the English peasant's lot was only slightly better than that of his Irish colleague because he tilled more fertile soil). To a great extent the landed classes (who, after all, surely had a *prima facie* interest in the survival of their tenants) were motivated by greed or hobbled by ignorance, not driven by some insane desire to see peasants die for the sport of it. And yet if one listened to some Irish people - most of them entirely ignorant of the facts - one could be forgiven for thinking that the potato blight was deliberately introduced into Ireland by the English in an attempt to exterminate them.

Secondly, landlord absenteeism is taken as an indication of a contempt for the Irish on the part of the English. Well, there were far more absentee Irish landlords than absentee English landlords, and the brutal question must be asked: if you, the reader, had had land holdings not only in the barren and miserable west of Ireland but also in the fertile east, or over in England, where would *you* have lived?

Even if the charge of deliberate genocide could be laid at a few landlords' doors, and even if a few of those landlords were English, then "the English" as a nation could still not be blamed for what went on. Indeed, it is well documented that the English population *as a whole* were appalled by the tales of suffering which eventually filtered through to England, and that they demanded that something be done about it forthwith. Grants were made by English churches, private donations were made, fasts were held in London in sympathy (not that fasting actually achieved anything, but it indicates the state of the English mind at this time). The American reformer Asenath Nicholson records in her *Annals of the Famine in Ireland* the following: "that the English people felt more deeply, and acted more consistently than did the people of Ireland (i.e. the Anglo-Irish Ascendancy), cannot be disputed". Nicholson also says "had [the English], without being advised or influenced in the least by the Irish landlords and Irish relieving-officers, taken their own course, much better management of funds and better management for the suffering would have followed". She continued (betraying a not altogether complete grasp of Irish history): "the English . . . never had oppressed these poor ones, while the rich, powerful Irish, like our slaveholders in the United States, had long held them writhing in their grasp . . . ".

The famine gave political impetus to Peel's repeal of the Corn Laws in 1846, which he proceeded with even though he knew it would bring down his government and split his party asunder. Peel also created public works, made government grants, pegged prices and distributed food in Ireland, in attempting to provide some relief from the dreadful suffering in what was, by then, simply another part of the United Kingdom. If his successor Lord John Russell's responses were less imaginative, it is still as pointless, misguided, and inaccurate to blame all Englishmen for what went on in the west of Ireland in the nineteenth century as it is to blame all Irish people for the antics of a few Irish terrorists in the twentieth.

It is surely anachronistic to still be harping on about all the alleged crimes of the English after all these years. Even in the matter of the original Cambro-Norman invasion, responsibility quite obviously lay on both sides, and has lain on both sides ever since. Irish history has been complicated by the admixture of religion with economics and politics, and complicated by the existence of the Anglo-Irish, who were "neither fish nor fowl". It is intellectually dishonest and absolutely pointless to attempt to apportion blame at this distance, and this behoves the myth-peddlers and the ill-informed to give their anti-English rhetoric a rest.

Scotland

Scotland's history vis-à-vis England is fundamentally less complicated than that of Ireland. Whilst there were incursions by both nations upon the other's territory, and various outrages perpetrated by both sides, there was no large-scale colonization, if one ignores the ancient and permanent colonization of southeast Scotland by the Northumbrian Anglo-Saxons long before Scotland existed as a nation, and if one also ignores the wide and permanent infiltration of Anglo-Norman nobles in the twelfth century. Members of these two groups are equivalent to the Old English in Ireland, in that they became completely Scottish in any realistic sense of the word centuries ago - after all, Robert Bruce was an Anglo-Norman, and who would not describe him as Scottish?! There has been no colonization of Scotland analogous to the Protestant colonization of Ireland, and Scotland remained effectively (if not always nominally) a foreign power until her union with England in 1707.

Ignoring the inevitable mixing of the races which has occurred in Scotland - especially since the Highland Clearances - the mainland Scots are two distinctly different races of people. The people of the north, west and centre are Pictish/Celtic, and the people of Lothian (the south-east) are basically Anglo-Saxon. The fact of south-east Scotland's ancient connections with

Anglo-Saxon and Norman England is crucial, and may well explain why Scotland's history vis-à-vis England did not follow a pattern similar to that of Ireland. The Scottish centre of political gravity had slipped down into Lowland Scotland by the time of the "war of independence" in the late thirteenth/early fourteenth century, all of Lowland Scotland had adopted Anglo-Norman language and institutions by that time, and the aristocracy had extensive family connections with the Anglo-Normans in England. David I (1124-53), the Anglicized son of an English mother, granted many baronies to Anglo-Norman friends from over the border, including members of the families which would later be known as the Bruces, the Balliols, and the Stuarts. He also set about deliberately replacing Celtic tribalism with Anglo-Norman feudalism, as best he could. He and his successors replicated the English shire system and the concept of the King's justice, and the Celtic die-hards who would not adapt gradually skulked away behind the Highland Line. Thus, the struggle between England and Scotland was never a racial one, but was a clash of two interrelated Anglo-Norman feudal kingdoms.

Edward I declared himself King of Scotland in 1296 on the basis of some typically feudal reasoning, and a long list of Scottish Anglo-Norman nobles (many of whom were hamstrung by having lands on both sides of the border) did him homage. Thus it was left to an obscure Scottish knight named William Wallace to fight the first rounds of the "war of independence". This war, fought under Wallace and Bruce, featured the only two military successes against the English which anyone can remember, those at Stirling Bridge and Bannockburn. Both were soon avenged by the English but, all myth-peddling aside, Bannockburn was an important victory for Scotland, since it secured her "independence". How continued overlordship by English kings in Scotland may have manifested itself, however, is a moot point. It should be considered that the English kings thought of their relationship with Scotland in traditionally feudal terms, rather than in the acquisitive way in which some of their subordinates viewed Ireland. Little practical effect "on the ground" was felt in most feudal relationships, where an overlord simply demanded fealty and service from his vassal, and placed a few yes-men at the vassal's court. The two countries may simply have drifted together sooner than they eventually did. Spice is added to any idle speculation as to how things might have turned out by consideration of the parallel nature of the two countries' subsequent histories. Within two hundred and fifty years of Bannockburn both England and Scotland had broken with Rome; within three hundred years they shared a *Scottish* king; and within three hundred and fifty years both countries had rebelled separately against that king's son, and had been briefly united under Cromwell's Commonwealth. Within four hundred years the flirting was finally over, and the reluctant spouses were finally married.

What, then, of "the Union"? Scottish nationalists would have us believe that the noble Scot suffocates still under an unjust and evil English yolk, and that Scotland is being held back from the brilliant destiny which would be hers if only the parasitic English would get off her back. Well, be that as it may, in 1707 Scotland was a basket case, and in desperate need of the free access to the markets of England and all her colonies which only union with England could give her. The Scottish Parliament passed the treaty effecting union with England voluntarily; it was not forced upon her by her substantially richer, more populous and more powerful neighbour.

This brings us to Scotland's most immortal myth, the Highland Clearances. It should be remembered that the backdrop to the Clearances was the Catholic Jacobite rebellions of 1715 and in particular of 1745, in which Bonnie Prince Charlie tried to revive the Stuart family's claim to his grandfather's two thrones.

Once again, the execrated Stuarts stalked the land, and British government forces were obliged to defend the precarious Protestant constitutional monarchy which England and Scotland now jointly enjoyed. Before the end of his ill-fated campaign, more Scottish clans and Scotsmen were against Charles Edward Stuart than were for him, and he never commanded more than ten thousand men, nor gained any significant support in the Protestant Lowlands or in England. It is not his ineffectual march into England, and the *denouement* at Culloden in 1746 at the hands of King George II's son the Duke of Cumberland, which need concern us here, but the ensuing circumstances by which many "Macs" and "Mcs" later found themselves living in foreign lands. The final failure of the Jacobites was followed by a long overdue eradication from British shores of the last vestiges of a recidivist, stone-age feudalism, and this much still seems reasonable, considering the ultra-dangerous circumstances of the time. The lands of Jacobite chiefs were expropriated, the personal legal jurisdiction of all surviving chiefs over their people was abolished, and the tribal relationship between chief and clan was replaced with a conventional landlord/tenant relationship. The British government provided the Highland chiefs with the hobnailed boot, but it was the surviving chiefs themselves who planted that boot firmly in the goolies of their clansfolk, kicking them off their lands for profit, renting the land out to graziers, and adopting the lifestyle of the aristocratic landlord (in some cases decamping to London). It should also be noted that most ministers of the Presbyterian Church provided vociferous support to the chiefs in what they were doing.

This is not to say that all of the chiefs behaved in this way, nor is it to claim that some new proprietors were not English, but many evictions were undertaken by ancient clan chiefs who now saw that there was more money in sheep farming than in loyalty to their kinsmen. However, before trying and condemning these chiefs in the name of every single descendant of a Highlander who now lives in Lowland Scotland, England, or anywhere else in the world, something else should be considered. Emigration from the Highlands certainly pre-dated the Clearances (and continues to this day), as Highlanders addressed themselves to the depressing economic realities of life in a cold, barren, rural backwater, and as they railed against the lack of upward social mobility inherent in a tribal system. There was growing commercial contact with the Lowlands from the beginning of the eighteenth century, and there is ample evidence of seasonal and permanent migration to the Lowlands and abroad from that time. Many Highlanders broke free of the repressive clan system on their own initiative (only later to romanticize it), and sought a new life elsewhere. Thus, not every citizen of the Anglo-Saxon countries who has a Highland surname can attribute their current location to their ancestors being cleared from the Highlands. However, of those who can, more than one must thank God (and the Duke of Cumberland) every day that their ancestors lost the Battle of Culloden, and that they were thus saved from living in some damp and miserable Scottish village all their lives, but instead find themselves living in Canada, America, Australia, New Zealand or even England (Heaven forbid).

Finally, a moment should be spent examining the "Cult of the Highlands" which has such a profound grip on the psyches of many Americans in particular, and colours the judgment of many people about Scotland as a whole. The Cult of the Highlands can be precisely dated to the royal visit to Scotland by George IV in 1822, at which time many Lowland lairds started to affect the dress and customs of the Highlanders whom their fathers and grandfathers had so feared and detested. At about the same time, most clan tartans were invented by various entrepreneurs and charlatans, to the enduring financial benefit of tartan manufacturers everywhere. The embarrassing and ironic habit of the British royal family sojourning in the Highlands each year also dates from the nineteenth century, when the German Queen Victoria and her German husband inaugurated that strange tradition. The author is not qualified to speak on behalf of Lowland Scots, but it may well irritate some of them - it certainly should - that "Scotland" is seen by many people as being synonymous with *Highland* Scotland, and that Highland bagpipes and the Braemar Gathering are considered to be what Scotland is all about, and that affecting the dress of Highlanders is considered the height of Scottish self-expression. On a good day, the Highlands cannot be beaten for scenic grandeur, but it is a poor and miserable area of the country, and it was an outdated tribal backwater by the time of the Jacobite rebellions. It was also a source of conservative resistance to the constitutional and economic progress which was well underway in the rest of Great Britain (including Lowland Scotland) by the middle of the eighteenth century. Life must have been perfectly miserable for most of its inhabitants, and the myths which now surround the Highlands are a typical example of anachronistic romanticization of a place by people who did not and do not have to raise a family there, and of a social system under which they did not and do not have to live.

Chapter 8

THE COLONIES AND EMPIRE

What of England's relationship with her colonies and empire? It should first be remembered that the English were not the only people in acquisition mode between the sixteenth and nineteenth centuries, and in the author's opinion there were far worse people to fall "victim" to than the English. It should be kept in mind that the countries colonized by the English were going to be colonized by someone: the Europeans had such a preponderance of economic and military power by the sixteenth century, and particularly during the seventeenth to nineteenth centuries, that colonization by a foreign power was irresistible in most cases. It therefore seems pointless to argue whether colonization *per se* is a good thing or not - the only question back then was: "who would it be"?

Let us not apologize for being the nation which turned out to be the best at colonization. But let us not be "holier than thou" about our colonization efforts, either. We did not do it for the benefit of the locals, we did it for our own - either for the personal financial benefit of individual colonists, or for England's strategic benefit. Only a dreamer completely out of touch with historical reality and human psychology would criticize anyone for that.

India

For all its many faults, British rule in India brought an almost unheard-of peace to the sub-continent, and carried in its train constitutional, social and economic progress which ultimately converted India from a patchwork of feudal and warring states into the world's largest (but perhaps most imperfect) democracy. By the time when Britain was gaining supremacy in India, that country had become an irredeemable mess of religious, racial and class intolerance - and it would appear that it has reverted back to being one since independence (actually it has become three separate messes, since Pakistan and Bangladesh also emerged out of "British India"). The Moghuls' uncertain authority over the many separate states in India was in disarray by the middle of the eighteenth century, and despite Pitt's India Act of 1784 forbidding aggressive war or annexation by the British East India Company, the company was unavoidably drawn into adjudicating or intervening in wars between competing Indian states. The early nineteenth century finally saw an acceptance of the inevitable by British politicians (stimulated by a paranoia about Russia's intentions to the north-west), leading to a series of acquisitive wars, and the sponsoring of "treaty states" which surrendered control of their foreign policy to Britain in exchange for protection from other Indian states. Complete supremacy was achieved by 1849, resulting in a patchwork of Indian states under overall British authority (although many remained under local Indian control right through to independence in 1947), many preferring British overlordship to rule by a competing Indian state. British rule in India should thus be attributed as much to the debilitating mutual hatreds and jealousies of separate Indian states, as to naked British imperialism.

America

Examination of Hollywood's current politically-correct output will reveal that the Red Indian as the "baddie" has been extinct since at least the beginning of the 1990s. Indeed, the cruel and greedy paleface (not all of whom were Anglo-Saxons, by any means) is now the standard baddie, and this may be no more than a fair re-balancing of the ledger. As one small example, let us examine the children's film *Pocahontas*, which concerns the English settlement of Virginia. An uninformed viewer of that film (i.e. any child) could be forgiven for thinking that the English were rapacious and arrogant aggressors (which they probably were!) and that the peace-loving American Indians had, until that moment, lived an idyllic lifestyle, at one with nature and each other, never prey to aggression, nor initiators of it. More about that laughable obfuscation in a moment.

New Zealand, Australia and Canada

Much is currently being said about the injustices and failures of British rule vis-à-vis the indigenous populations of New Zealand, Australia and Canada, and the impression could be taken that the Maori, Aborigines, and Inuit would have been much happier if they had been left well alone. Well, maybe; maybe not. The point is that the alternative to British rule was not the Maori, Aborigines, and Inuit continuing to go about their stone-age businesses unmolested, but New Zealand, Australia and the whole of Canada being run by the Dutch or French. Maybe the Indonesians and Algerians should be asked for their opinions as to the attractiveness of those alternatives.

South Africa

Anglo-Saxon South Africans must take their fair share of responsibility for the many crimes of the distant past, and the many apartheid-era crimes which have recently been examined by Bishop Tutu's Truth and Reconciliation Commission. Nevertheless, any improvements in the blacks' circumstances which did take place during the long and generally unsympathetic period of white rule, such as the freeing of the Boers' black slaves in the 1830s, were initiated by the British, not the Boers. Therefore, the question must be asked: would the black South Africans seriously have wanted the Boers - the architects of the apartheid system - in sole charge over the last two hundred years? Probably not.

Commentary

So, what is to be said to the revisionists who would have us believe that every indigenous race from Maori to American Indians lived in peace and harmony before the English came, at one with nature and their neighbours, never raping, enslaving and murdering, nor being raped, enslaved or murdered? Even a feeble grasp of world history, and an amateur understanding of human nature would suggest that the chances of such an idyllic lifestyle having been the norm are, shall we say, slim. Every race known to man has had its quota of violent thugs, sadists, crooks, cowards, bullies, wife-beaters, child-abusers, rapists, free-loaders, charlatans, whores and lunatics, and the author cannot think of any reason why that would not have been the case amongst these stone-age peoples, who kept no written records by which such a theory can be proven or disproved.

The implication of the revisionists' claims is, of course, that the English spoiled everything, and caused the indigenous races to fall from Grace. The coming of the English is implied or stated to have been an unequivocally Bad Thing - and in the author's opinion, for all the English's crimes, follies and injustices, such a claim is arrant nonsense. For sure, the English committed many crimes and perpetrated many injustices, but in this regard they were no different from any other conqueror (be that a conqueror from the next village, or a conqueror from the other side of the world). Indeed, the author believes that any dispassionate reading of history shows that the English were rather more benign, over all, than the average conqueror.

Colonization was an extremely hazardous occupation, and carried with it great risks. In the first place, many colonists never even made it to their destination, perishing at sea by storm or shipwreck, or (in earlier years) by enemy action or at the hands of pirates. Those who did make it lived a precarious existence: many lost everything to famine and failure, many others were carried off by disease (for example the first Governor of New Zealand, William Hobson RN, who died in office from some form of paralytic fever, probably contracted in the West Indies). Others were killed by natives (for example, Captain James Cook RN, killed and eaten by cannibals in the Hawaiian Islands). It is surely understandable, therefore, that under the strain of these risks British colonists might have sometimes been a little robust in their handling of some of the natives whom they came across - in any case, it can be assumed that the natives intended to be every bit as robust back!

Nor should the apparent arrogance of these colonists be taken out of context. However much the modern liberal might deplore it, it must certainly have seemed to white colonists that they came from "superior" civilizations. Take as an example Captain Cook, who has been criticized for an allegedly arrogant attitude towards the Maori; firstly it should be pointed out that Captain Cook is well known for having been one of the more humane and enlightened of European explorers of the colonial era. However enlightened he might have been, though, it must have been difficult not to feel a little, shall we say "advanced", being as he was an officer in the service of a nation which had just destroyed the imperial ambitions of its only serious rival, and being as he was the subject of a nation which was rapidly industrializing and outstripping all others in wealth and power. What is more, he arrived upon the shores of New Zealand as a navigator who had just sailed right around the world, and as the commander of a comparatively massive ship armed with cannon and muskets, to find himself in the presence of a stone-age people whose largest vessel was a canoe, and whose deadliest weapon was a club.

It is time for the English to be proud of their heritage, and not be ashamed of their ancestors.

Conclusion

CONCLUSION

This royal throne of kings, this scepter'd isle,
This earth of majesty, this seat of Mars,
This other Eden, demi-paradise,
This fortress built by Nature for herself
Against infection and the hand of war
This happy breed of men, this little world,
This precious stone set in the silver sea,
Which serves it in the office of a wall,
Or as a moat defensive to a house,
Against the envy of less happier lands,
This blessed plot, this earth, this realm, this England

Shakespeare, Richard II

So, there stands England; plenty of blemishes to be sure, but a fine and significant record nevertheless.

It might be objected by those wishing to "knock" England that most of this is history - which indeed it is. And yet, a country's history enters the fabric of its society: just as a person's character is formed by his or her background and experiences, so is a nation's. England's history of lawfulness, freedom, parliamentary democracy, "fair play", heroic deeds, innovation and leadership has entered into the character of the English people (wherever they now live), if the author is not mistaken, and is very much part of what the words "English" or "Anglo-Saxon" have come to mean. There is usually a grain of truth in the generalizations which develop about peoples, over time. In the case of the English, when any bigotry and prejudice on the part of those expressing an opinion have been stripped away, the generalizations about the English actually tend to be quite favourable.

Some resent us; others admire us; but few can ignore us. To be sure, England is no longer the most powerful nation on earth, nor the richest, but she has been those things - which is something that very few nations can claim. She stood for two centuries at the core of the most widespread, the richest, the most powerful and, for all its many injustices, the most just empire in history. As she has done from the beginning, she remains the predominant country within the United Kingdom, and even on her own England would still be a rich, powerful and influential nation. Her capital city is a world-scale centre for finance, insurance, banking, fine art, diamond trading, oil trading, fashion, the music industry, air travel, publishing, entertainment, jewelry, and a host of other things. London is also home to a host of international administrative, sporting and theological organizations such as the Commonwealth, the International Cricket Council, and the Anglican Church.

England had a great empire and now she has none. In this regard, she is no different from all the other great empires which have ever existed. However, the manner in which the second British empire was dismantled is where England perhaps parts company from the rest, since it was essentially an orderly and peaceful process in most cases - especially in the Anglo-Saxon dominions and in India (despite some disorder in the latter territory). This is perhaps best attested to by the fact that so many of the former British colonies are members of the Commonwealth. To be sure, self-interest plays a large part in any decision to become a member of an organization like the Commonwealth, but the fact remains that if the British had been universally detested rulers, then one might think that newly sovereign states would have found continued association with

Britain unpalatable. England's reputation amongst her former colonies and dominions compares favourably to the reputation of the other European colonial powers in their former colonies, or to Japan's reputation in China, or China's in Tibet, or Indonesia's in East Timor, for example.

England has left many indelible marks upon the broader world, both in her own right and as the predominant part of Britain and the United Kingdom. All who are British can be proud of some of the achievements discussed in this book, but the English can be proud of them all. This includes people of English extraction whose ancestors long since emigrated to such places as America, Canada, Australia, New Zealand, and South Africa. Even those Americans and Canadians who can (or claim they can) trace their ancestry to the first English settlers in America had ancestors in England when Magna Carta was signed, when English common law and the jury system developed, and when the English Church split with Rome. Even those Kiwis, Australians and White Africans who can (or claim they can) trace their ancestry to the earliest direct English settlement of their lands had ancestors in England when all four of the great milestones of English constitutional history were laid down, and when the Industrial Revolution commenced. The ancestors of many other citizens of these five Anglo-Saxon countries, who emigrated much later than with the "first fleets", were present in England throughout her two greatest centuries.

Amongst the many things for which England is responsible, some are of fundamental importance, some are merely noteworthy, and some may seem trivial, but everyone on earth is affected by them, to one degree or another. The indelible marks which England has left upon the world would include, in no particular order:

Parliamentary Democracy

This is not unique to England, of course, but the English constitutional system is the model for many constitutions the world over - for example, the English constitutional arrangements in place by 1701 were the model for the American Constitution, and the American system inspired the French. The constitutional system of England has played a pivotal role in the development of England, and in the development of all nations with an historic connection to England. More than one and a half billion people live under constitutional arrangements derived or descended from England's constitution;

English Common Law, Trial by Jury, and "The Rule of Law"

The English legal system has been transplanted all around the world. Trial by jury has receded in the non-Anglo-Saxon countries and in South Africa, but England's common law remains, sometimes synthesized with religious jaws, and sometimes synthesized with native customs. It has developed a life of its own in the United States, and has been merged with civil law in such places as Scotland, the Philippines, Quebec, Louisiana and South Africa. "The rule of law" is not unique to England of course, but England generally circumscribed the absolute powers of her rulers somewhat earlier than was done elsewhere, and transplanted her characteristic way of doing things through due process of law to her colonies (as and when the exigencies of each local situation permitted). England's constitutional arrangements, especially her parliamentary democracy and the vital jury system (which has many times served as a pressure-release valve), gave rise to an early tradition of tolerance and peaceable agitation rather than revolution, and this goes a long way towards explaining the English character, and the process of England's and her colonies' histories;

A General Tradition of Freedom and Liberty

It is easy for the cynic to sneer at such a claim, but despite her failings in this area (including those implicit in the very fact of conquest and rule over any other country), it must still be acknowledged that the tenor of England's history is liberal. Amongst many other things, England is responsible for the concept of *Habeus Corpus* being part of many legal systems around the world. Britain also led the fight against the slave trade, led the world in moves towards free trade and the amelioration of working conditions in factories, abolished suttee and female infanticide in India, and spawned the world's first trade union movement and cooperative societies;

The English Language

Spoken as a mother tongue by around four hundred million people, and spoken to some degree or another of proficiency by over one billion people. English is, in effect, the world's lingua franca;

Sports

Cricket, rugby, badminton, squash and standardized rules for soccer, tennis, hockey and boxing, and the seeds of American football and baseball. In short, the most loved games in the world, enjoyed by billions of people when they are all added together, have either been invented by the English, or have had their rules and regulations laid down by them; and

Various Other Things

Such as the Greenwich Meridian and Universal Time, against which all locations and time zones are referenced - on the surface of the earth, in the sky, and in space; the industrial revolution; the Church of England; driving on the left side of the road; the Salvation Army; the Scout and Girl Guide movements; and a whole host of other good things.

For those people living in places like America, Canada, Australia and New Zealand, manifestations of England's history are everywhere around them - the language they speak, and many of their idioms; their place names; their constitutional systems; their legal systems; the faith most of them adhere to; and so on. In every other country in the world, England's history manifests itself in the sports they play; their longitude; their time zone; the language they probably employ to communicate with foreigners; and so on. There must be very few places on earth which have not yet been affected by England's history in one way or another. Of course, there may be some unknown race of tribesmen still living deep in a jungle somewhere who have as yet had no contact with the outside world, but when they do they will soon find England's story weaving its way into their lives too. If their leaders deem it appropriate to develop some constitutional arrangements, they may well model their system on England's or America's, and in either case they will thus immediately be affected by English history. Even if this does not happen, their location and time zone will be fixed with reference to Greenwich; their leaders will probably find it convenient to learn English one day; and their schoolboys will probably learn to kick footballs around in conformity with the accepted rules of the game. You can run, but you can't hide from England's history.

Scotland, Wales, Ireland

What of the Scots, Welsh and Irish? They display admirable pride in their heritages - and why not? Cultural pride is something the author understands and applauds, although it should be said that kilts, Welsh hymns and Irish jigs seem faintly ridiculous when worn, sung or jigged by residents of foreign lands who may be only one-eighth the race in question, and seven-eighths Anglo-Saxon.

For sure, Wales, Scotland and Ireland have played their respective roles in the history of Britain and the United Kingdom, and the author is not suggesting otherwise. However, it should be kept in mind that the population of England is about ten times that of Scotland, ten times that of the whole of Ireland (North plus Republic) and seventeen times that of Wales. Overall, the combined population of Wales, Scotland and Ireland (North plus Republic) amounts to about one-fifth the total population of the United Kingdom plus the Republic of Ireland. Thus, the roles of the Scots, Welsh and Irish have always been relatively minor, made more minor by the fact that the government has operated from London, and has always been dominated by Englishmen. In any case, most of the developments which have been discussed in these pages are specifically English - it is not Scottish law which has been dispersed across the English-speaking world; it is not the Gaelic nor Welsh languages which around four hundred million people speak as their first language, and the rest of the world uses as their *lingua franca*; it is not rules developed in Scotland, Wales or Ireland which have become the accepted international law for a dozen sports; and it is not the Edinburgh nor Dublin nor Cardiff Meridians which all vessels, aircraft, satellites and spacecraft plot their position against. Where shared credit *can* be claimed - for example, the industrial revolution - then the vast majority (but not all) of the credit is still due to England.

And while we are on the subject of Scotland, Wales and Ireland, let the English not be ashamed of their history vis-à-vis these peoples either. Whatever the true facts surrounding England's alleged heinous crimes and injustices, that was the nature of the times in which our ancestors lived: life *was* "nasty, brutish and short", and the Scots, Welsh and Irish would most assuredly have done the same things to us (and occasionally did) if we had not done them better and more often to them.

Arise, England!

Some Final Thoughts

As has already been stated, "the English nation" comprises not only all Anglo-Saxons who have lived, or are now living, in England or anywhere else in the world (regardless of their modern-day citizenship), but also a few non-Anglo-Saxons who became or have become "English" through naturalization and long domicile in England. "English" men and women have been settling in foreign lands for four hundred years now, and their direct descendants live all over the world, but particularly in the United States, Canada, New Zealand, Australia, South Africa, and Ireland. Many other English men and women never ventured abroad, and played their roles in England's story from their green and pleasant homeland. Wherever they lived and died, the collective effect of "the English nation" upon the world has been extensive and profound.

There is quite possibly at least one set of English bones interred in every country in the world, but the graves of English men and women are to be found in particularly large numbers in Africa, the Indian sub-continent, South-East Asia, Ireland, North America and the Pacific. They can be found on deserted shorelines, in jungles, in deserts, in frozen wastelands, on fertile plains, and in little English cemeteries all around the world. The passing of the centuries and the action of rain, mildew, frost, sand, or sun have long since rendered many of their headstones unreadable, or have rotted or bleached the little wooden crosses which may have served in their stead. The final resting places of some other Englishmen were only ever marked by a pile of stones, others by nothing at all - including the "graves" of some who fell in battle, and all those who were buried or lost at sea. All of these people were members of the English family, and whether each individual is long forgotten or still remembered, and whether they were much mourned or their loss was lamented by no one, their massive collective legacy endures.

A country's history is formed and defined not only by its notables but also by its unseen masses, and the character of a nation is an inscrutable admixture of the characters and history of all of its people, through all of time. Every English man and woman who has ever lived, through sixty generations spanning fifteen hundred years, has played some part in England's admirable history, and if the reader is English by birth or naturalization, or is a descendant of English ancestors, then whoever the reader may be, whatever their current citizenship, wherever they may live, and whatever their ancestors' backgrounds, they should be proud of their history: it is world-scale, and it is a good one.

Truly it can be said that:

The whole earth is the tomb of English people,
and their story is not graven only on stone over clay,
but abides everywhere,
woven into the stuff of other people's lives.

Appendix A

Reigns of the Kings and Queens of England

Anglo-Saxon period (notables only)

Hengist and Horsa	mid 5th cent.	Reputedly the leaders of the first Saxons in England
Edwin	616-632	Northumbria
Oswald	633-641	Northumbria
Oswiu	641-670	Northumbria
Ethelbald	716-757	Mercia
Offa	757-796	Mercia
Alfred	871-899	Wessex
Edward the Elder	899-924	Wessex
Athelstan	924-939	Wessex. The first king of all England
Ethelred the Unready	979-1016	Wessex
(Danish Interlude)	1016-1042	
Edward the Confessor	1042-1066	Wessex
Harold II	1066	Godwin

Conquest to Elizabeth II

William I	1066-1087	By conquest. Died in harness. Succeeded by son:
William II	1087-1100	Died while hunting (poss. murder). Succeeded by brother:
Henry I	1100-1135	Died in harness. Succeeded by nephew:
Stephen	1135-1154	Died in harness. Succeeded by his cousin's son:
Henry II	1154-1189	Died in harness. Succeeded by son:
Richard I	1189-1199	Died in harness. Succeeded by brother:
John	1199-1216	Died in harness. Succeeded by son:
Henry III	1216-1272	Died in harness. Succeeded by son:
Edward I	1272-1307	Died in harness. Succeeded by son:
Edward II	1307-1327	Usurped by wife and son. Put to death. Succeeded by son:
Edward III	1327-1377	Died in harness. Succeeded by grandson:
Richard II	1377-1399	Deposed by:
Henry IV	1399-1413	Ratified by Parliament. Died in harness. Succeeded by son:
Henry V	1413-1422	Died in harness. Succeeded by son:

Henry VI	1422-1461	Deposed by Edward IV
	1470-1471	"Re-adepted", then deposed again. Put to death.
Edward IV	1461-1483	Ratified by Parliament. Died in harness. Succeeded by son:
Edward V	1483	Murdered by persons unknown. Succeeded by uncle:
Richard III	1483-1485	Last king of England to die in battle. Deposed by:
Henry VII	1485-1509	Ratified by Parliament. Died in harness. Succeeded by son:
Henry VIII	1509-1547	Died in harness. Succeeded by son:
Edward VI	1547-1553	Died in harness (aged 16). Succeeded by half-sister:
Mary I	1553-1558	Died in harness. Succeeded by half-sister:
Elizabeth I	1558-1603	Died in harness. Succeeded by aunt's great-grandson:
James I	1603-1625	Ratified by Parliament. Died in harness. Succeeded by son:
Charles I	1625-1649	Deposed by Parliament. Executed. Succeeded later by son:
	(Interregnum)	
Charles II	1660-1685	Died in harness. Succeeded by brother:
James II	1685-1688	Fled to France. Replaced by daughter and son-in-law:
William III	1688-1702	Died in harness. Succeeded by sister-in-law:
(& Mary II)	1688-1694	(Executive authority in William's hands).
Anne	1702-1714	Died in harness. Succeeded by grandfather's great-nephew:
George I	1714-1727	Died in harness. Succeeded by son:
George II	1727-1760	Died in harness. Succeeded by grandson:
George III	1760-1820	Died in harness (incapable from 1812). Succeeded by son:
George IV	1820-1830	Regent from 1812. Died in harness. Succeeded by brother:
William IV	1830-1837	Died in harness. Succeeded by niece:
Victoria	1837-1901	Died in harness. Succeeded by son:
Edward VII	1901-1910	Died in harness. Succeeded by son:
George V	1910-1936	Died in harness. Succeeded by son:
Edward VIII	1936	Abdicated. Succeeded by brother:
George VI	1936-1952	Died in harness. Succeeded by daughter:
Elizabeth II	1952-	

Appendix B

Certain clauses of Magna Carta, 1215

The clauses of Magna Carta considered most important from a constitutional point of view (or otherwise of special interest) are reproduced below. Note that the charter was re-issued several times, but it soon became clear that keeping it up to date was going to be impracticable, and so it quickly became more a statement of basic principles, than a statement of extant law. In any case, constitutional historians consider that it is not the letter of the charter which has mattered to English history, but the spirit.

John, by the grace of God, king of England, lord of Ireland [etc. etc.], to the archbishops, bishops, abbots, earls, barons, justiciars, foresters, sheriffs, stewards, servants, and to all his bailiffs and faithful subjects, greeting. Know that we, out of reverence for God and for the salvation of our soul and those of all our ancestors and heirs, for the honour of God and the exaltation of holy church, and for the reform of our realm, on the advice of [Stephen Langton, Archbishop of Canterbury, and twenty-six other named parties], and others, our faithful subjects:

1. In the first place have granted to God, and by this our present charter confirmed for us and our heirs for ever that the English church shall be free, and shall have its rights undiminished and its rights unimpaired; and it is our will that it be thus observed; which is evident from the fact that, before the quarrel between us and our barons began, we willingly and spontaneously granted and by our charter confirmed the freedom of elections which is reckoned most important and very essential to the English church, and obtained confirmation of it from the lord Pope Innocent III;

the which we will observe and we wish our heirs to observe it in good faith for ever. We have also granted to all free men of our kingdom, for ourselves and our heirs for ever, all the liberties written below, to be had and held by them and their heirs of us and our heirs.

12. No scutage [money paid in lieu of feudal service] or aid [grant of subsidy or tax to the king] shall be imposed in our kingdom unless by common counsel of our kingdom, except for ransoming our person, for making our eldest son a knight, and for once marrying our eldest daughter, and for these only a reasonable aid shall be levied. Be it done in like manner concerning aids from the city of London.

13. And the city of London shall have all its ancient liberties and free customs as well by land as by water. Furthermore, we will and grant that all other cities, boroughs, towns, and ports shall have all their liberties and free customs.

14. And to obtain the common counsel of the kingdom about the assessing of an aid (except in the three cases aforesaid) or of a scutage, we will cause to be summoned the archbishops, bishops, abbots, earls and greater barons [etc. etc.] - for a fixed date, namely, after the expiry of at least forty days, and to a fixed place; and in all letters of such summons we will specify the reason for the summons. And when the summons has thus been made, the business shall proceed on the day appointed, according to the counsel of those present, though not all have come who were summoned.

15. We will not in future grant any one the right to take an aid from his free men, except for ransoming his person, for making his eldest son a knight, and for once marrying his eldest daughter, and for these only a reasonable aid shall be levied.

17. Common pleas [civil actions, not amounting to a breach of the peace] shall not follow our court, but shall be held in some fixed place.

20. A free man shall not be amerced [fined, punished] for a trivial offence except in accordance with the degree of the offence, and for a grave offence he shall be amerced in accordance with its gravity, yet saving his way of living; and a merchant in the same way, saving his stock-in-trade; and a villein shall be amerced in the same way, saving his means of livelihood - if they have fallen into our mercy; and none of the aforesaid amercements shall be imposed except by the oath of good men of the neighbourhood.

21. Earls and barons shall not be amerced except by their peers, and only in accordance with the degree of the offence.

28. No constable or other bailiff of ours shall take anyone's corn or other chattels unless he pays on the spot in cash for them or can delay payment by arrangement with the seller.

30. No sheriff, or bailiff of ours, or anyone else shall take the horses or carts of any free man for transport work save with the agreement of that free man.

31. Neither we nor our bailiffs will take, for castles or other works of ours, timber which is not ours, except with the agreement of him whose timber it is.

38. No bailiff shall in future put anyone to trial upon his own bare word, without reliable witnesses produced for this purpose.

39. No free man shall be arrested or imprisoned or disseised [dispossessed] or outlawed or exiled or in any way victimised, neither will we attack him or send anyone to

attack him, except by the lawful judgment of his peers or by the law of the land.

40. To no one will we sell, to no one will we refuse or delay right or justice.

41. All merchants shall be able to go out of and come into England safely and securely and stay and travel throughout England, as well by land as by water, for buying and selling by the ancient and right customs free from all evil tolls, except in time of war and if they are of the land that is at war with us. And if such are found in our land at the beginning of a war, they shall be attached without injury to their persons or goods, until we, or our chief justiciar, know how merchants of our land are treated who were found in the land at war with us when war broke out, and if ours are safe there, the others shall be safe in our land.

42. It shall be lawful in future for anyone, without prejudicing the allegiance due to us, to leave our kingdom and return safely and securely by land and water, save, in the public interest, for a short period in time of war - except for those imprisoned or outlawed in accordance with the law of the kingdom and natives of a land that is at war with us and merchants (who shall be treated as aforesaid).

45. We will not make justices, constables, sheriffs or bailiffs save of such as know the law of the kingdom and mean to observe it well.

60. All these aforesaid customs and liberties which we have granted to be observed in our kingdom as far as it pertains to us towards our men, all of our kingdom, clerks [clerics] as well as laymen, shall observe as far as it pertains to them towards their men.

61. Since, moreover, for God and the betterment of our kingdom and for the better allaying of the discord that has arisen between us and our barons we have granted all these things aforesaid, wishing them to enjoy the use of them unimpaired and unshaken for ever, we give and grant them the under-written security, namely, that . . . if we, or our justiciar, or our bailiffs or any one of our servants offend in any way against anyone or transgress any of the articles of the peace or the security . . . [the Barons] shall petition us to have the transgression corrected without delay. And if we do not correct the transgression [the Barons] together with the community of the whole land shall distrain and distress us in every way they can, namely, by seizing castles, lands, possessions, and in such other ways as they can, saving our person and the persons of our queen and our children, until, in their opinion, amends have been made; and when amends have been made, they shall obey us as they did before.

63. Wherefore we wish and firmly enjoin that the English church shall be free, and that the men in our kingdom shall have and hold all the aforesaid liberties, rights and concessions well and peacefully, freely and quietly, fully and completely, for themselves and their heirs from us and our heirs, in all matters and in all places for ever, as is aforesaid. An oath, moreover, has been taken, as well on our part as on the part of the barons, that all these things aforesaid shall be observed in good faith and without evil disposition. Witness the above-mentioned and many others. Given by our hand in the meadow which is called Runnymede between Windsor and Staines on the fifteenth day of June, in the seventeenth year of our reign [1215].

This translation: Encyclopaedia Britannica, 15th Edition, © 1998, Volume 7, pages 674-676

Appendix C

BRIEF NOTES ON SOME FAMOUS ENGLISH BATTLES

The battles sketched below are described as "English" battles because they were fought predominantly by English soldiers and sailors, and were initiated and/or led by English kings or a predominantly English Parliament. However, it should be noted that battles subsequent to 1707 generally involved some Scottish soldiers as members of the British forces, and that battles subsequent to 1801 also generally involved Irish soldiers (most notably the Duke of Wellington, who was Anglo-Irish). Welsh soldiers fought for England as early as the fourteenth century, in particular as archers in the first three battles mentioned. Note that the first four battles discussed below did not contribute in any way to the worldwide dissemination of England's story, but are included for their historical interest nonetheless.

Halidon Hill (1333)

If you trace the Anglo-Scottish border from west to east, it follows a nondescript path until over the Cheviot hills, whereupon it drops down to the River Tweed and follows that river almost to the North Sea coast. A short distance from the sea it suddenly cuts away from the river and runs north, skirting the town of Berwick-upon-Tweed on its western and northern sides, thus leaving that town a part of England. The Anglo-Scottish border has been this anomalous shape since the Battle of Halidon Hill in 1333.

Halidon Hill lies just north-west of Berwick, and the battle fought there is noteworthy for two reasons. Firstly, it was one of the most one-sided battles in history; and secondly, it was at

Halidon Hill that Edward III witnessed for himself the awful potentialities of the long-bow, which he later employed to equally devastating effect at Crecy.

The question at issue in 1333 was whether Balliol (Edward III's nominee) should be restored to the throne which he had seized the previous year, or whether Robert Bruce's infant son David, for whom Lord Archibald Douglas was Regent, should succeed his father.

In brief the battle consisted of companies of Scottish spearmen slithering through some marshy ground at the bottom of Halidon Hill and then labouring up the slope towards three divisions of archers, behind whom lurked the hardly necessary English cavalry and spearmen. As soon as they came into range, the Scots were winnowed by the archers, and the few exhausted survivors who made it to the top of the hill were simply hacked to bits by the fresh English cavalry. Simple, really.

Thus did Berwick become English, and Balliol become King again. The Regent Lord Douglas was killed, as were six Scottish earls, seventy Scottish barons, five hundred Scottish knights and squires, and thousands of Scottish foot-soldiers. The English lost fourteen men.

Crecy (1346)

The root cause of the Hundred Years' War was the existence of two conflicting claims to the throne of France. Following the death of Charles IV in 1328, Philip of Valois claimed the Crown as the nephew of Charles' father Philip IV but Edward III of England claimed it as the son of Philip IV's daughter. A council of French nobles elected Philip, and Edward initially accepted this decision, and swore loyalty to the first Valois king.

However, in due course Edward repudiated his oath on the grounds that he had been a minor at the time, and the war began in 1337. By that time the French should have been fully aware of the potentialities of the English longbow, because they should have heard reports of the Battle of Halidon Hill (see above). Even if they had not, by 1346 the French had *themselves* witnessed its effects elsewhere, but still had not adapted their tactics accordingly.

Edward took up a standard defensive position at Crecy, and awaited attack. Philip's ill-disciplined army came into view at about 6 p.m., and certain elements of it broke ranks and immediately charged the English. Philip was obliged to follow immediately, rather than have his force disintegrate. The English were first attacked by an advance guard of Genoese cross-bowmen, and shortly after the Genoese had loosed an ineffectual volley at the English, the English returned the compliment with a maelstrom of arrows - it is estimated that sixty thousand arrows were loosed at the Genoese in one minute (implying a firing rate of one arrow per eight seconds per archer). Nothing like so concentrated a barrage had ever been seen before, and the Genoese who did not die on the spot began to flee back towards the advancing French cavalry, who proceeded to ride them down. Throughout the mayhem which ensued, aggravated by a second wave of French cavalry colliding with the stalled first wave, the English continued to pour their arrows into the French army with impunity.

Hand to hand combat took place at the fringes of the battle, but the battle was, in principle, fifteen consecutive head-on French cavalry charges, each mowed down by a storm of English arrows. Philip eventually withdrew, leaving two dead kings on the battlefield (the kings of Majorca and Bohemia); one thousand five hundred and forty two lords and knights; and countless foot soldiers.

The only direct English gain which followed from the victory at Crecy was Calais, which was captured the following year and held until 1558, but this gain was a vital one as it provided a bridgehead into Europe through which English cloth and wool passed unimpeded for two hundred and eleven years.

Agincourt (1415)

Henry V invaded France in 1415 with the modest aim of regaining for England the entire Angevin empire (amounting to about two-thirds of France). At Agincourt he found his way blocked by a French army of about twenty five thousand men, outnumbering his own force by three to one. This imbalance of forces, and awareness that many of the English had been laid low by dysentery, produced a lamentable over-confidence amongst the French hierarchy.

Henry and the French Dauphin faced each other for four hours, until Henry advanced his army to within three hundred metres of the French, and goaded the French with arrows. Eventually the French responded, by cavalry charge from the French army's two flanks, and by dismounted cavalry advance in the centre. Apparently, no one in France had read up on the Battle of Crecy, because Agincourt was basically a repeat performance. The French were subjected to the traditional sky-darkening hail of English arrows; their cavalry swerved inwards under this barrage and collided with their dismounted cavalry, and the whole colossal traffic-jam was simply slaughtered from long range by the archers. The chaotic mess slowly made its way into contact with the English centre, whereupon the archers threw down their bows and piled into the stalled melee with axe and dagger, and murdered anyone they could find who was still alive.

The French lost at least ten thousand men, including many of the greatest nobles of France, to England's five hundred.

> And gentlemen in England, now a-bed
> Shall think themselves accurs'd they were not here
> And hold their manhoods cheap whiles any speaks
> That fought with us upon Saint Crispin's day.

Shakespeare, Henry V

Henry proceeded from Agincourt to ultimately occupy all of Normandy, and the later Treaty of Troyes betrothed him to the French king's daughter, and made him the acknowledged heir to the French Crown.

Flodden (1513)

The Battle of Flodden, in Northumberland, was the last major action of war fought between the English and Scottish nations. It was fought as a result of an invasion of England by James IV of Scotland in support of his French allies, whom Henry VIII was at that time attacking in France. In Henry's absence, the English forces were led by Thomas Howard, Earl of Surrey.

The opposing armies were of similar size, both being in the region of thirty thousand strong at the time of engagement. Problems started for the Scots when James' ill-disciplined left wing broke under artillery fire, and charged Howard's right wing, to no great effect. James was obliged to follow his left wing down from the high ground, but stalled in the face of English artillery and archers. The English slowly ground James' centre to a pulp, and decimated his right flank from a distance, with archers.

When the Scots decide it's time for a defeat again, they don't go in for half measures. On this occasion, something like ten thousand Scots died, probably outnumbering the English dead by ten to one. James IV was killed, along with ten earls, thirteen barons and ninety heads of clans.

Commentary

As was stated above, these first four battles pre-date the worldwide dissemination of England's story and they have been included here only for their historical interest. On the other hand, the first of the battles below (the Boyne) secured the Glorious Revolution, and the battles which follow it are some of Britain's most famous of the eighteenth and nineteenth centuries. Each of them contributed directly to Britain's rise to a position of undisputed world power and influence in those centuries.

The Boyne (1690)

The Battle of the Boyne was fought near the town of Drogheda on Ireland's east coast, north of Dublin. The battle is aptly named, since a good deal of the action actually took place *in* the River Boyne! Both contending kings were present on the battlefield: King James II at the head of about twenty thousand primarily Irish and French troops, and King William III (who was wounded on the day) at the head of about thirty thousand primarily English and Dutch troops.

The Irish would have been better advised to withdraw west of the Shannon River and harry the English by guerrilla warfare, but chose to make a stand west of Drogheda, and so lined themselves up on the south bank of the river, facing north.

The English decided upon the rather unpromising tactic of fording the river under fire, with a view to joining battle with the Irish on the south bank.

The battle commenced with the English right wing attempting to cross the river at a bridge near the village of Slane. After a stiff fight they were able to do so, while William swam his horse across the river at the head of his left wing, and the English infantry waded across in the centre. The Irish infantry were able to do only limited damage to, and were unnerved by the resolution of, the approaching English centre, and they quickly disintegrated and fled. The Irish cavalry resisted for a while longer, but the battle was effectively decided by William's safe arrival on the south bank, and after some desperate fighting by the Irish and French cavalry, the Irish army was routed.

The Glorious Revolution of 1688 was secured by the flight of James II to France after this battle, and an uncertain authority in Ireland was established by the English, made more secure by the Battle of Aughrim the following year.

Blenheim (1704)

The Battle of Blenheim shifted the European balance of power decisively in favour of England, at the expense of France. It was fought in south-west Germany between an English-Savoyard army under John Churchill (the first Duke of Marlborough) and a Franco-Bavarian army under Louis XIV (who was not present).

Churchill's march from the Channel coast to Blenheim is almost as famous amongst military historians as the actual battle, being a logistical masterpiece in which he dodged and bluffed the French time and time again. The battle itself was a conventional enough affair, consisting of a mile-wide head-on assault against the French line preceded by the neutralisation of the two fortified villages of Blenheim and Oberglau, between which the main French force was positioned.

The separate battles which raged in and around the two villages as a prelude to the main assault appeared for a long time to be headed for stalemate. However, something was being achieved from Churchill's point of view, because the French centre was slowly bled of reserves, to bolster the defence of the villages. Ultimately the French centre became so weak that it was unable to withstand Churchill's main assault by eight thousand cavalry and fifteen thousand infantry, which smashed it decisively and carried the day. It is said that when the French commander who had been responsible for the redeployment of the reserves away from the centre saw what he had done, he rode his horse into the Danube and drowned himself.

Allied losses were twelve thousand killed or wounded, to enemy losses of around thirty nine thousand killed or wounded.

Plassey (1757)

The Battle of Plassey is noteworthy for two reasons: it effectively secured British ascendancy in India, which turned out to be of monumental importance; and it was an otherwise trivial little skirmish, costing twenty three English dead and less than five hundred of the enemy.

A showdown between the armed British East India Company and the Nawab of Bengal, Surajah Dowlah, was made inevitable by the incarceration by him of somewhere between sixty four and one hundred and forty six British prisoners (depending on whose account one believes) in the "Black Hole of Calcutta" in 1756.

The cell in question measured fourteen by eighteen feet, and only about twenty two prisoners survived the night.

Lieutenant-Colonel Robert Clive, in charge of British forces in the region, perceived that an alliance between Dowlah and France was in the offing, and conspired with the Nawab's commander-in-chief, Mir Jafar, to depose him. In return for a promise of all French bases in Bengal plus Calcutta, Clive agreed to help Jafar depose Dowlah.

Clive advanced upon Dowlah, and encamped his small army of about three thousand men at the village of Plassey. The following day he drew his forces up in the open against fifty thousand Bengalis, but after suffering some light casualties from artillery, withdrew to a mango orchard from where his men slowly mowed down several hundred of the advancing enemy. An enemy commander charged the orchard but was killed, whereupon his men panicked and fled. Jafar advised Dowlah to leave the field, whereupon the leaderless Bengalis rapidly disintegrated and were put to flight by the small British force.

Jafar was installed as a puppet of the British, and thus did British rule in India commence.

Quebec (1759)

In 1759, France was too heavily occupied fighting the British in Europe to be able to assist her forces in Canada, and they were left very much to their own devices. Pitt the Elder sent General Wolfe to assault Quebec as part of a three-pronged attack on the French forces in Canada.

The French commander Montcalm made two fundamental mistakes. First, he believed that the St. Lawrence could not be navigated beyond Quebec, but this was disproved by, amongst others, a young Naval officer by the name of James Cook, who turned out to be quite a good navigator. Secondly, he believed that an attack must come from the eastern side of the town, since the Plains of Abraham to the south were protected by a two hundred foot cliff.

Therefore, Wolfe had his troops ferried by the Royal Navy beyond Quebec, and then scaled the cliff in the dark with about five thousand men, and drew them up on the Plains. Montcalm hurried into battle with about an equal number of men, but the British carried the day. In the course of the fighting, both the thirty two year old Wolfe, and Montcalm were killed.

Quebec was occupied, and the whole of Canada was ceded to Britain at the end of the Seven Years' War.

Minden (1759)

The Battle of Minden was a decisive battle of the Seven Years' War, but is also noteworthy for the suicidal bravery of the British infantry which defied all accepted military logic by defeating cavalry without support.

As a result of a misunderstood order (which is something of a tradition in the British Army), six British infantry regiments set off at a march straight towards the massed cavalry in the centre of the French army. As they approached, French artillery assailed them, but to the French commander's amazement they kept coming. Eleven squadrons of French cavalry were therefore dispatched towards the front three regiments of British infantry, but these were completely destroyed by a single volley of massed fire, stopping them as if they had hit a brick wall. A further fourteen squadrons were then sent as a second wave, and received similar treatment. During this time, a notable act of cowardice was perpetrated by Lord Sackville, commander of the British cavalry - he refused a direct order to ride out and support the infantry. Sackville was court-martialled and dismissed the service for this act, and he was lucky: Admiral John Byng had been shot - as Voltaire put it *pour encourager les autres* (to encourage the others) - for failing to break the French siege of Minorca three years earlier.

Further cavalry and infantry attacks by the French were repulsed by the British, and by a Hanoverian regiment alongside them, under support from the British artillery. In essence, the British infantry simply refused to be beaten, and eventually the French were routed, despite their superiority in numbers, and driven from the field.

Victory at Minden ensured the survival of England's only ally in Europe, Frederick the Great, and this was of paramount importance since had he succumbed, England would have faced an entire Continent united against her.

Quiberon Bay (1759)

The third great victory of 1759 was won at sea on the afternoon of 20 November, on a lee shore (the wind blowing towards the shore), under a rising westerly storm.

In these extremely hazardous conditions, and without pilots, Admiral Hawke's twenty seven capital ships chased twenty one French capital ships into the shallows of Quiberon Bay on the west coast of France, following them closely, and relying on the French fleet's local knowledge to keep both fleets off the rocks.

The French rearguard was overhauled and several ships were

captured or destroyed before nightfall. The British fleet anchored overnight, during which time two British ships and several French ships (including their flagship) ran aground and were all destroyed. Several other French ships jettisoned their cannon to reduce their draught, and escaped over a shallow bar into the Vilaine Estuary.

The French lost seven capital ships to enemy action or foundering, to England's two run aground, and the French fleet was thereafter bottled up under close blockade for the remainder of the Seven Years' War. This cut their communications with Canada and India, and removed the risk of a French invasion of England.

The Nile (1798)

The Battle of the Nile was fought on the night of 1-2 August 1798 between two fleets at anchor.

A French fleet of thirteen capital ships under Admiral Brueys was anchored line-ahead under a light northerly wind, in Aboukir Bay at the mouth of the Nile. There was land and shallows to the west of the fleet, and Brueys believed that no enemy ships could get "inside" his ships on the landward side. He was wrong. Lord Nelson's eleven ships sailed into the bay from the north, ran down both sides of the French line, and anchored by their sterns alongside their chosen adversaries. When each ship had pummelled its adversary into submission, she then raised anchor and re-positioned herself alongside her next selected victim. Thus the English fleet slowly worked its way down the line of French ships, and had utterly destroyed it by daybreak.

The French lost eleven capital ships, with two escaped

(Villeneuve, the loser at Trafalgar, was a notable escapee). Three thousand two hundred French sailors were killed or wounded (to English casualties of about one thousand), and another three thousand were taken prisoner. The French army in Egypt was thereby cut off from France, stymieing Napoleon's Eastern ambitions, and Britain again took control of the Mediterranean.

Trafalgar (1805)

The Battle of Trafalgar was fought off the coast of Spain on 21st October 1805, under a light north-westerly wind.

Villeneuve's allied French and Spanish fleet of thirty three capital ships (of which fifteen were Spanish) was formed broadly in line-ahead, sailing north, when engaged by Lord Nelson from the west. Nelson had split his attacking force of twenty seven capital ships into two columns, the northerly commanded by himself, and the southerly commanded by Collingwood.

Battle commenced just before noon when the first ship to reach the enemy, *Royal Sovereign* under Collingwood, engaged the Spanish *Santa Anna*. Before long, action was general, as each English ship pierced the Allies' line at her chosen spot, and wore up alongside the enemy. Admiral Nelson was mortally wounded at around 1.15 pm., but lived long enough (until about 4.30 p.m.) to learn that he had won his last and most famous victory.

The allied French and Spanish fleet lost eighteen capital ships, of which seventeen were captured by the British. Two thousand six hundred enemy sailors were killed or wounded, and another seven thousand were taken prisoner. The British fleet lost no capital ships, and suffered one thousand seven hundred casualties.

This crushing victory gave impetus to the formation of the fourth coalition against Napoleon, and it gave Britain unlimited command of the seas for the remainder of the Napoleonic wars. This effectively brought French maritime trade to a standstill; completed the process commenced at the Nile of confining Napoleon to Europe; caused Napoleon to abandon his plans for the invasion of England; and allowed England to prosecute the war on the Spanish Peninsula, which drained French resources and gave hope to her other foes.

Footnote: An ordinary seaman wrote home after this battle as follows (quoted by Warner, see bibliography):

> "I never set eyes on him [Nelson], for which I am both sorry and glad, for to be sure I should like to have seen him, but then, all the men in our ship who have seen him are such soft toads, they have done nothing but blast their eyes and cry ever since he was killed. God bless you! Chaps that fought like the devil sit down and cry like a wench".

Now *that's* leadership!

Salamanca (1812)

As we have seen, the Battle of Trafalgar enabled Britain to pursue the war against Napoleon through Portugal and into Spain, with considerable strategic implications. The Peninsular War was an ulcer for Napoleon, draining men and equipment away from his central European campaigns.

One of the Peninsular War's most noteworthy battles was fought at Salamanca, where Wellington came out of his normal defensive mode (in which he was an acknowledged master, and much respected by the French marshals). In this battle, the French commander Marmont was caught on the hop by Wellington, because he assumed that Wellington would remain true to form and not take the offensive, but would always wait to be attacked.

Thus when Marmont spotted a cloud of dust to his west-northwest on the morning of the battle he believed it to be the British Army moving away from him (westwards) to a new position. Therefore, he dispatched three divisions of his troops in a westerly direction, to march parallel and to the south of the assumed track of the British, with orders to overtake and attack them. Unfortunately for him he was wrong (it was a division of the British forces heading due south out of Salamanca!), and he was therefore hit badly in the flanks of all three divisions by that force, and by other Anglo-Portuguese forces rapidly deployed by Wellington from behind screening hills. The British infantry and cavalry effectively ambushed the French divisions, wiping out a quarter of the French troops within the first thirty minutes of the battle, wounding Marmont and killing his replacement.

The battle was decisive, liberating Madrid and weakening the French hold on Spain. Wellington's reputation was also pushed sky-high amongst the French (and as Britain's problems with Rommel in the Second World War would demonstrate, enemy generals' reputations are an important matter). Campaigning in the following year, combined with the debilitating effects of the Spanish guerrilla warfare which was much encouraged by such victories as Salamanca, led to the Spanish Peninsula falling effectively into complete allied control by the end of 1813, opening the way over the border into France.

Waterloo (1815)

Napoleon escaped captivity on Elba in 1814, and returned to Paris in triumph. It thus became clear that only total military defeat would rid Europe of him, for which purpose an allied force of Anglo-Dutch soldiers under Wellington, and Prussian soldiers under Blucher, was assembled.

After initial skirmishes two days before, the allies and the French came face to face, for the last time, on 18th June 1815. Wellington took up a defensive position south of Waterloo, facing south, and left it to Napoleon to take the initiative. The French fielded about seventy two thousand men and Wellington fielded about sixty eight thousand.

Napoleon delayed his attack to allow the ground to dry, and made his main thrust, in a northerly direction, in the centre at about 1.30 p.m. This was repulsed, as were further cavalry assaults, by which time (about 4 p.m.) Blucher's men were arriving in dribs and drabs from the east to bolster the British left flank. Withdrawal was now the prudent course but Napoleon risked all with a further assault on Wellington's centre by the Imperial Guard, which suffered the same fate as his earlier efforts. The repulsing of the Imperial Guard broke morale in the French ranks, and Wellington ordered a general advance upon the enemy. Napoleon withdrew from the field, finally defeated, and Blucher's Prussians chased off the remnants of his beaten army.

Napoleon's final defeat was followed by his second abdication, and his imprisonment on St. Helena deep in the South Atlantic, where he died in 1821.

Commentary

Many of the victories from the Boyne to Waterloo were stunning in themselves, and all were decisive and deserve to be remembered. The list of British victories in the eighteenth and nineteenth centuries is seemingly endless, but no purpose would be served by examining more than the handful selected. The battles above are some of the most famous of them all, and each had great strategic importance in the building of the British Empire, and of British prestige.

Nor were victories lacking in the twentieth century, of course, but by then the British Empire was on the wane. Therefore, the many heroic deeds performed by British and allied servicemen in the twentieth century did not contribute to the worldwide dissemination of England's story in the way that the battles just discussed did.

NOTES

[1] Unless otherwise stated, dates given for rulers are dates reigned, not dates of birth and death. See Appendix A for a list of the most notable Anglo-Saxon kings, and a list of all English monarchs since 1066.

[2] The terms *Angevin* and *Plantagenet* are interchangeable, and refer to the English kings from Henry II (1154-89) to Richard II (1377-99). Angevin means "of Anjou" (Henry II's father was Geoffrey of Anjou), and the *plante genet* (broom) was the family's emblem.

[3] These paragraphs draw upon an article published by the New Zealand Herald written by Gwynne Dyer, London-based journalist and historian. Dyer's article itself draws upon work by Bryn Walters, of the Association of Roman Archaeology.

BIBLIOGRAPHY

Brooke, C., "The Saxon and Norman Kings", Fontana Library, 1967

Chrimes, S.B., "English constitutional History", Oxford University Press, 1967

Claiborne, R., "English - its Life and Times", Bloomsbury Publishing Ltd, 1994

Crystal, D., "Cambridge Encyclopedia of Language", Cambridge University Press, 1997

Fisher, H.A.L., "A History of Europe", Fontana, 1982

Foster, R.F., "The Oxford History of Ireland", Oxford University Press, 1989

Fraser, A. (Ed.), "The Lives of the Kings & Queens of England", Weidenfeld & Nicolson, 1975

Fulbrook, M., "A Concise History of Germany", Cambridge University Press, 1992

Goubert, P., "The Course of French History", Routledge, 1991

Jolly, R., "Jackspeak", Palamanando Publishing, 1989

Kitto, H.D.F., "The Greeks", Penguin Books, 1988

MacKay, A., "Spain in the Middle Ages", The MacMillan Press Ltd, 1977

MacLean, F., "Highlanders", Viking Penguin, 1995

Markham, F.M.H., "Napoleon", The New English Library Ltd, 1963

Mason, R.H.P, and Caiger, J.G., "A History of Japan", Charles E Tuttle Inc., 1973

McCrum, R. et al, "The Story of English", Faber and Faber Ltd/BBC Books, 1988

Morgan, K.O., (Ed.), "The Oxford History of Britain", Oxford University Press, 1993

Murphy, M. (Ed.), "Asenath Nicholson: Annals of the Famine in Ireland", Lilliput Press Ltd, 1998

New Encyclopaedia Britannica, 15th edition, Encyclopaedia Britannica Inc., 1998

Oxford English Dictionary, 7th edition, Oxford University Press, 1988

Passant, E.J., "A Short History of Germany 1815-1945", Cambridge University Press, 1962

Pemsel, H., "Atlas of Naval Warfare", Lionel Leventhal Ltd, 1977

Prebble, J., "The Lion in the North", Penguin Books, 1981

Regan, G., "Famous British Battles", Michael O'Mara Books Ltd, 1997

Richards, E., "A History of the Highland Clearances", Croom Helm Ltd, 1985

Ridges, E.W., "Constitutional Law of England", Stevens and Sons, 1905

Roberts, J.M., "The Penguin History of the World", Penguin Group, 1995

Russell, P.E. (Ed.), "Spain", Methuen & Co., 1973

Smelser, M. and Gundersen, J.R., "American History at a Glance", Barnes & Noble, 1975

Suetonius (trans. Graves, R; revised Grant, M), "The Twelve Caesars", Penguin, 1989

Trevelyan, G.M., "A Shortened History of England", Penguin Books Ltd, 1959

Trevor-Roper, H., "The Rise of Christian Europe", Thames and Hudson, 1966

Warner, O., "A Portrait of Lord Nelson", Penguin Books, 1987

Wolpert, S., "A New History of India", Oxford University Press, 1989

INDEX

Academie Francais	82
Act of Settlement (1701)	69
Act of Union (1707)	31
Act of Union (1801)	35
Agincourt, Battle of	162
Alfred the Great	48
American Football	97
Anglican Church (see Church of England)	
Anglo-Irish "Ascendancy"	125
Anglo-Irish Treaty	41, 119, 120
Anglo-Saxons	20, 49, 50, 52
Aragon	59, 63
Association Football (see Football)	
Aughrim, Battle of	35, 165
Australia	32, 40, 41, 42, 137
Baden-Powell, Lord	111
Badminton	96
Bank of England	29
Bannockburn, Battle of	130
Baseball	97
Berwick-upon-Tweed	159
Bill of Rights (1688)	68, 102
Black Hole of Calcutta	166
Blenheim, Battle of	165
Boer War	41
Boers	40, 138
Booth, William	111
Boxing	96
Boy Scouts	111
Boyne, Battle of	35, 164
British Army	85, 96
British East India Company	37, 39, 74, 136, 166
Bruce, Robert	30, 129, 160
Burnswater	51
Byng, Admiral John	169
Cabal	70
Cabinet System	70, 75
Caesar, Julius	19
Calais	162
Cambridge Rules (Soccer)	92
Canada	32, 38, 40, 41, 42, 137
Cape of Good Hope	40
Castile-Leon	59, 63
Catholic Church	22, 23
Celts	19
Censorship	102
Charles I	26, 66
Charles II	27, 28, 67, 99
Chaucer	79
China	60, 63, 74
Christianity	20
Church of England	65, 110, 144
Civil (Roman) Law	48, 62, 76
Civil War, English	27
Clare, Richard de (see Pembroke, Earl of)	
Claudius	19
Clinton, Bill	70
Clive, Robert	39, 167
Clontarf, Battle of	34
Colonial Office	40
Commons	26, 57, 60, 61, 62
Commonwealth	42, 144
Cook, James	40, 139, 168
Cooperative Movement	107
Corn Laws	104, 128
Crecy, Battle of	160
Cricket	93
Cromwell, Oliver	27, 35, 38, 123
Cromwell, Richard	27
Culloden, Battle of	132
Cumberland, Duke of	132, 133
Dail Eireann	120
Danelaw	20, 52
Danes	30
David I	130
Delhi Sultanate	60
Dermot, King of Leinster	120
Drake, Francis	24, 37
Driving on the Left	108
East Midland Dialect	78, 79
Easter Uprising	41
Edward I	25, 48, 56, 57, 130
Edward III	160
Edward VII	72

Edward the Confessor 20, 24
Elizabeth I 24, 64, 110
Elliot, Sir John 66
Ellis, William Webb 94
English Bible 79
English Common Law 28, 48, 55, 62, 76
English Constitution 49
English Language 78
Enlightenment 105
Estates General 59, 62, 63, 73
Female Infanticide 106
Female Suffrage 76
Feudalism 52
FIFA 93
Flodden, Battle of 163
Football 92
Football Association 92
Football League 92
France 22, 32, 62, 73, 82
Frederick the Great 169
Free Trade 32, 104
Freemen 51, 56
French Revolution 49, 73, 75
Gambia River 38
George III 33
George IV 133
Germany 32
Ghana 43
Gibraltar 32, 38
Girl Guides 111
Glorious Revolution 31, 68, 165
Government of Ireland Act (1920) 120
Greenwich Meridian 99, 100
Greenwich Observatory 99, 100
Gunpowder Plot 26
Habeus Corpus 103
Habeus Corpus Act (1679) 103
Halidon Hill, Battle of 159
Hawke, Admiral Edward 169
Henry II 48, 52, 53, 101, 120
Henry III 56
Henry IV 79
Henry V 162
Henry VI 60
Henry VII 64
Henry VIII 22, 23, 64, 163
Highland Clearances 129, 131, 133

Highlands, Cult of the 133
Highland Question 33
Hobson, William RN 139
Hockey 95
Holland 38
House of Commons 61, 67, 69
House of Lords 27, 61, 69, 76
Howard League for Penal Reform 106
Howard, John 106
Howard, Thomas, Earl of Surrey 163
Hudson Bay 39
Hudson's Bay Company 38
Huguenots 28
Hundred Years' War 21, 62, 79, 160
Impeachment 70
Imperial Conference 41, 42
Imperial Cricket Conference 93
India 32, 37, 42, 60, 63, 74, 82, 135
India Act (1784) 39, 136
Indian Mutiny 41
Industrial Revolution 33, 109
International Cricket Council 93, 144
Ireland 34, 41, 58, 62, 72, 119-129
Irish Famine 127
Irish Free State 41, 42
Irish Home Rule 125
Jacobites 31, 33, 131, 132
Jamaica 38
James I and VI 25, 26, 62
James II 28, 68, 164
James IV 163
Japan 60, 63, 74
John, King 55, 56
Jury-of-Verdict 52, 53, 54, 73, 76
Justices of the Peace 55
Kentish Dialect 78
Kildare, Earls of 124
Knox, John 31
Labour Party 107
Langton, Stephen 55
Licencing Act (1586) 102
London 55, 144
London Prize Ring Rules 97
London Stock Exchange 109
Lothian 129
Louis XIV 28, 38, 67, 165
Louis XV 73

MacAlpin, Kenneth 30
Magna Carta 53, 55, 66, 102, 103
Maori 137, 138, 139
Marcher Lords 24
Marlborough, Duke of 28, 32, 165
Marx, Karl 107
Mary, Queen of Scots 24, 31
Marylebone Cricket Club 93, 95
Meiji Restoration 60
Mercia 20
Mercian Dialect 78
Minden, Battle of 33, 168
Ministry System 71
Minorca 32, 38, 169
Mir Jafar 167
Moghul Empire 39, 63, 74, 136
Montfort, Simon de 56
Napoleon 54, 108, 172, 174
Napoleonic Wars 40, 71
Nelson, Lord Horatio 84, 85, 170, 171
New Zealand 40, 41, 42, 76, 137, 139
Nicholson, Asenath 128
Nile, Battle of 170
Normandy 21, 55
Normans 20, 24, 34, 48, 52, 79, 120, 121, 129, 130
Northern Ireland 35, 41, 120, 123
Northumbria 20, 29
Northumbrian Dialect 78
Old English, the 121, 122, 123, 126
O'Neill, Hugh 123, 124
Orange Free State 41
Orange, William of (see William III)
Parlement 59, 73
Parliament 26, 28, 57, 60, 64, 67, 68, 70, 75, 79
Patrick, Saint 123
Peel, Robert 86, 128
Peine Forte et Dure 51
Pembroke, Earl of 34
Peninsular War 172
Petition of Right (1628) 26, 65, 66, 102
Pitt, William the Elder 167
Pitt, William the Younger 35
Pitt, Thomas 38
Plassey, Battle of 33, 39, 166
Pope Clement VII 23
Pope Gregory VII 22
Pope Innocent III 53

Prayer Book 79, 110
Presbyterian Church 62, 132
Quebec, Battle of 33, 167
Queensberry Rules 97
Quiberon Bay, Battle of 33, 169
Raffles, Sir Stamford 40
Raleigh, Sir Walter 37
Redistribution Act, 1885 76
Reform Act, 1832 75
Reform Act, 1867 75
Reform Act, 1884 75
Reformation 23, 65
Renaissance 22, 62
Romans 19, 108
Rome 22, 23, 64
Roses, Wars of the 21, 64
Rotten Boroughs 32, 75
Rounders 97
Royal Navy 23, 26, 83, 99, 168
Rugby Football 94
Rugby Football League 94
Rugby Football Union 94
Rugby School 94
Russell, Lord John 128
Salamanca, Battle of 172
Salvation Army 111
Saxons 50, 51
Scotland 29, 58, 62, 129-134
Scots 30, 123, 124, 129, 149
Scottish Rebellion 67
Scottish Reformation 24, 31
Serfdom 74
Seven Years' War 33, 39
Sierra Leone 105
Singapore 40
Slave Trade 104, 105
South Africa 41, 42, 137
Spain 22, 59, 73
Spanish Armada 24
Spanish Inquisition 63
Spanish Succession, War of the 32, 38
Squash 95
Standard Time 100
Star Chamber 54, 67
Statute of Westminster (1931) 41, 42
Stirling Bridge, Battle of 130
Stuart, Charles Edward 131, 132

Stuarts	65
Surajah Dowlah	166
Suttee	105
Tennis	95
Thegns	52
Thirty-Nine Articles	110
Tory Party	70
Trade Unionism	106
Trades Union Congress	107
Trafalgar, Battle of	34, 171
Transvaal	41
Trial by Ordeal	53
Troyes, Treaty of	163
Ulster (see Northern Ireland)	
United Irishmen	35
United States	74, 82, 136
United States, Constitution of	49, 69, 74, 103
Utrecht, Treaty of	39
Victoria, Queen	41, 134
Virginia	38
Voltaire	169
Wales	24
Wallace, William	30, 130
Walter, Hubert	54
Waterloo, Battle of	34, 174
Wellington, Duke of	159, 173, 174
Wessex	20
West Saxon Dialect	78
Whig Party	70
Wilberforce, William	105
William III	29, 68, 164
Wolfe, General James	167
Wycliffe, John	79
Young Pretender (see Stuart, Charles Edward)	